When Hope and Fear Collide

Arthur Levine
and Jeanette S. Cureton
· ·

When Hope and Fear Collide

A Portrait of
Today's College Student

Jossey-Bass Publishers
San Francisco

Jossey-Bass books and products are available through most bookstores. To contact Jossey-Bass directly, call (888) 378-2537, fax to (800) 605-2665, or visit our website at www.josseybass.com.

Substantial discounts on bulk quantities of Jossey-Bass books are available to corporations, professional associations, and other organizations. For details and discount information, contact the special sales department at Jossey-Bass.

 Manufactured in the United States of America on Lyons Falls Turin Book. This paper is acid-free and 100 percent chlorine-free.

Credits are on page 188.

Library of Congress Cataloging-in-Publication Data

Levine, Arthur.
    When hope and fear collide : a portrait of today's college
student / by Arthur Levine and Jeanette S. Cureton.
        p.   cm.
    Continues: When dreams and heroes died.   1980.
    Includes bibliographical references and index.
    ISBN 0-7879-3877-7 (alk. paper)
    1. College students—United States.   2. College students—United
States—Attitudes.   3. College Students—United States—Political
activity.   4. Education, Higher—Social aspects—United States.
I. Cureton, Jeanette S.   II. Levine, Arthur.   When dreams
and heroes died.   III. Title.
LA229.L423   1998
378.1'98'0973—dc21   97-42414

FIRST EDITION
HB Printing   10 9 8 7 6 5 4

The Jossey-Bass
Higher and Adult Education Series

. . . .

97761

Contents

To our families: our spouses,
Bryant Cureton and Linda Fentiman;
and our daughters,
Elizabeth Cureton, Brown University, Class of '95;
Sarah Cureton, Mount Holyoke College, Class of '97;
Jamie Levine, Carleton College, Class of '01;
and Rachel Levine, Class of '08

Preface

In 1980, Arthur Levine wrote a book titled *When Dreams and Heroes Died*. It was a portrait of the college students of the late 1970s, based on national surveys and interviews of undergraduates and college administrators conducted by the Carnegie Council on Policy Studies in Higher Education.

The picture that emerged was of a generation optimistic about their personal futures but pessimistic about the future of the country. Students had adopted what might be described as a *"Titanic* ethic," a belief that they were being forced to ride on a doomed ship called the United States (or the world). But so long as the ship was afloat, they were determined to make the voyage as luxurious as possible and go first class.

With this outlook, students turned inward, focusing increasingly on "me." They became more vocationally oriented, with an emphasis on careers in the platinum professions: business, law, and medicine. Material goods assumed a greater importance in their lives. Two out of three students said it was essential or very important for them to be very well off financially.

Students reported the key social and political events that shaped their generation were Vietnam and Watergate. For three out of four undergraduates, the effect of these events was profoundly negative; they caused students to reject politics, political involvement, and government. When asked who their heroes were, "no one" topped the undergraduates' lists, followed distantly by God, entertainers, and athletes.

Student political attitudes grew more conservative than those of their predecessors, with increasing proportions favoring the death penalty, less coddling of criminals, and cessation of school busing. Nonetheless, student activism persisted on campus. One in five undergraduates reported having participated in a demonstration. But the issues shifted from prior years; instead of civil rights and Vietnam, students now protested over college costs and financial aid, faculty and staff hiring and firing, institutional facilities, and administrative policy. The agenda shifted from national to local issues and from social policy questions to consumer concerns.

Academically, students were entering higher education less well prepared in basic skills. Even so, they were getting higher grades in college than their predecessors. In growing proportion, undergraduates were selecting majors in the professions rather than the liberal arts. And they were taking more of their courses in their majors than in the past.

Socially, the feeling of community declined on college campuses, while individualism became more dominant. Self-interest clubs and groups proliferated, with a focus on gender, race, religious, and ethnic differences. Team sports diminished in popularity; individual sports grew. Students became more liberal about social issues, particularly those emphasizing individual rights and freedoms; they were more supportive than students in past years of premarital sex, legalization of marijuana, and liberalization of divorce laws.

These findings were a surprise to Levine. (We apologize that, in spite of our distaste in listening to Bob Dole refer to himself as Bob Dole during the 1996 presidential campaign, it seems best when talking about only one of the two authors of this book to use the third person.) He had not begun the research expecting to reach such conclusions—indeed, he probably resisted them.

Nonetheless, the portrait that emerged from the research was so upbeat and gladdening to the heart that Levine decided to continue the student interviews. Each year, he would visit more than a dozen campuses around the country. During the 1980s, he asked undergraduates on those campuses the same set of questions he had for the Carnegie Council studies. They kept giving him the same set of answers, with the notable exception that the proportion saying it was essential or very important to be very well off financially kept rising.

That is, until 1990. Then the answers started changing dramatically in such basic areas as optimism about the future, social involvement, and life goals. It was like flipping a light switch, so sudden was the change. At first, Levine dismissed the differences, chalking them up to having selected unrepresentative institutions, having arrived at a college at a strange moment, or having talked with an atypical group of students. But the differences persisted. Levine found them at colleges and universities across the country. Undergraduate attitudes, values, and beliefs appeared to be changing, and he wanted to find out how and why.

With this goal in mind, Levine repeated the Carnegie Council research of a decade and a half earlier. Jeanette Cureton joined him in planning and carrying out the research. In summer and fall 1992, they surveyed a nationally representative sample of 270 chief student affairs officers. In 1993, with support from the Lilly Endowment, a similarly representative sample of ninety-one hundred undergraduates was surveyed. These students were of both traditional and nontraditional age, as were the undergraduates of the earlier Carnegie studies. In addition to the 1993 survey, interviews were conducted from 1993 to 1995 with student body presidents, student newspaper editors, more chief student affairs officers, and small focus groups of students (averaging eight to ten in number and diverse in age, gender, and ethnicity) on twenty-eight campuses across the nation, selected to reflect the variety of American higher education. In 1995, the student newspaper editors and study body presidents were interviewed once again. In 1997, a chief student affairs officer survey was conducted one last time. Appendix A offers additional details on each of these studies, as well as others that were part of the research.

This volume is the product of that research. It seeks to paint a portrait of the current generation of college students. This is by no means a unique task; trying to capture the contemporary under-graduate in print has become a cottage industry of sorts.

Chapter One of this book examines popular conceptions of today's college students. The aim is to go beyond the caricatures and stereotypes to examine how the world in which current under-graduates grew up is different from that of previous students—demographically, socially, economically, globally, and technologi-cally. They've grown up in a time in which seemingly everything is changing.

The second chapter looks at the social and political world of today's undergraduates. It discusses the key social and political events that students say shaped their generation: the *Challenger* explosion, the Persian Gulf War, the decline of communism, the *Exxon Valdez* oil spill, AIDS, and the Rodney King trial. It exam-ines how these events have caused students to come to distrust the nation's social institutions, reject traditional politics, and turn away from well-known political leaders. Student politics defies traditional labels of liberal and conservative; it is issue oriented and rooted in a desire for change. Once again, undergraduates have heroes, and students are more socially active than at any time since the 1960s.

The focus shifts in Chapter Three to campus politics, in which we describe a world where consumerism is a growing reality. Stu-dents are acting increasingly as buyers and treating colleges more as sellers of a product. Student activism is on the rise, but participation in college governance is in decline. As undergraduates search on campus for a place to call home, their clubs are dividing into smaller and smaller groups based on race, ethnicity, gender, and sexual ori-entation, just to name a few differentiations. Campus politics is increasingly being shaped by these smaller affinity and self-interest groups.

Chapter Four examines the state of multiculturalism on campus. It is a painful topic, which students have a difficult time discussing. Minority students feel marginalized. Majority students are confused and uncertain about how to respond. Campuses are growing more and more voluntarily segregated. Undergraduates describe themselves in terms of their differences, not their commonalities. They systematically underestimate the degree of interaction between minority and majority students. There is a widespread sense of victimization among students.

Chapter Five is concerned with college social life. What students do for fun has changed little over time: drinking, parties, sports, music, and movies remain popular. But students have changed dramatically. More of them work at jobs, for longer hours, attend college part-time, and live off campus. Indeed, the campus is no longer the principal venue for student social life. Undergraduates are also coming to college more damaged psychologically. Binge drinking is on the rise, and traditional dating has all but disappeared from social life. Students are more socially isolated, have little time for social life, and are afraid of getting hurt.

Academics is the focus of Chapter Six. Today's undergraduates are career oriented. Their vocational concern is translated into their choices of college, majors, and long-term educational aspirations. Most students say they work hard, but there is a tendency to confuse hard work with being intellectual. Either way, the payoff is excellent, because current students are receiving the highest grades ever recorded as grade inflation continues to rise. Yet this comes at a time when students require greater levels of remedial education than their predecessors did. There is also a growing mismatch between the ways in which faculty teach and students best learn. Even so, student satisfaction with their academic experience has never been higher.

The seventh chapter deals with student hopes and aspirations for the future. Belief in the American dream is stronger than ever. Students want good jobs, financial success, meaningful relationships, and a family. Although they are optimistic, they are also scared— everything seems to be falling apart. They worry that they will be unable to find jobs, afford a family, be able to pay back their student loans, or even avoid moving back home with their parents.

The final chapter is a conclusion seeking to put the current student portrait into historical perspective. It examines what is new and what is old. It discusses the predictable cycles that undergraduates have undergone generationally. Current students do not fit this pattern. Instead, they are found to be a transitional generation in an era of historical discontinuity. We offer recommendations on the education that can best serve the current generation of young people.

Acknowledgments

This book would not have been possible without the help of a great many people. We are particularly grateful to Ralph Lundgren and the Lilly Endowment for funding this project. Without their support, this book could not have been written.

Jana Nidiffer worked with us on all aspects of this project from 1992 to 1994. We cannot think of any part of this project in which she was not involved during that period; she was an indispensable partner and we cannot thank her enough. Daphne Layton helped to plan this project and engaged in the earliest campus visits in the months after completing her doctorate before accepting a job at the University of Massachusetts. Nobody asks harder or better questions; she was much missed as the research progressed. Silverio Haro gave his all for this project. Seduced by the topic, he was forced to spend weeks learning different software and hardware applications to analyze portions of our data. We are also grateful to Inge-Lise Ameer, who filled in on a campus visit when desperately needed; Jack Carroll and the Opinion Research Corporation of Princeton, who administered the 1993 undergraduate survey; and Jan Civian, who helped with our data analysis. Sharon Singleton deserves special credit. She coordinated all aspects of the project from its start through 1994 and somehow kept all of us and all of the activities on track. We still don't know how she did it, but we do know she was wonderful to work with.

In 1994, when Arthur Levine moved from Harvard to Teachers College and Jeanette Cureton relocated to the Chicago area, a new cast of characters joined the project. Nancy Griffing, Jacquie Spano, and Kathy Shin took on the administration of the study. How they managed to perform the transition—juggling people, mountains of data, and logistics of all sorts without missing a beat—absolutely amazes us. To help during this second stage, two other individuals proved invaluable by retrieving much-needed information: Mary Jean Whitelaw of the Carnegie Foundation, who went out of her way to locate and interpret archived data; and librarian Donna Goodwyn of Elmhurst College, who became captivated by the project as she helped to uncover newer but even more elusive data.

Grace Tsai, a Teachers College student, carried out the 1995 study of student body presidents and newspaper editors. Kevin Kinser, a doctoral student at TC, served as our general research associate, keeping our research up to date and designing and directing the 1997 Student Affairs Survey. He was a lifesaver and a wonderful collaborator who added richly and substantially to our work; no one made a larger contribution to the project than Kevin.

To all of these friends and colleagues, we are more grateful than we can ever express. We also want to thank the chief student affairs officers in the Harvard Institute of Educational Management Class of 1992, who piloted the 1992 student affairs questionnaire. We thank as well the student affairs professionals who helped us redesign the survey for administration in 1996–97. And we are particularly grateful to the individuals who coordinated the twenty-eight campus site visits. Their names and institutional affiliations at the time of the original studies can be found in Appendix B. Finally, we want to express our gratitude to each of the hundreds of colleges and universities that agreed to participate in this study and the thousands of individuals who gave hours of their time for interviews and surveys.

January 1998

Arthur Levine
New York City
Jeanette S. Cureton
Elmhurst, Illinois

The Authors

• •

Arthur Levine is president and professor of education at Teachers College, Columbia University, in New York City. He received his bachelor's degree from Brandeis University and his Ph.D. from the State University of New York at Buffalo. Prior to Teachers College, he served as a senior faculty member and chair of the Institute for Educational Management at the Harvard Graduate School of Education.

Levine is the author of dozens of articles and reviews. His most recent book is *Beating the Odds: How the Poor Get to College* (with Jana Nidiffer), published in 1996. Among his other volumes are *Higher Learning in America* (1993); *Shaping Higher Education's Future: Demographic Realities and Opportunities, 1990–2000* (with associates, 1989); *When Dreams and Heroes Died: A Portrait of Today's College Student* (1980); *Handbook on Undergraduate Curriculum* (1978); *A Quest for Common Learning* (with Ernest L. Boyer, 1981); *Opportunity in Adversity* (with Janice Green, 1985); and *Why Innovation Fails* (1980). A 1982 Guggenheim Fellowship winner, Levine has received other awards as well, including the American Council on Education's Book of the Year award in 1974 (for *Reform of Undergraduate Education*); the Educational Press Association's awards for writing in 1981, 1989, and 1990; the National Association of Student Personnel Administrators' research award; the Council of Independent Colleges' academic leadership award; and thirteen honorary degrees. For a decade he was executive editor of *Change* magazine, and he

has served as a consultant to more than 250 colleges and universities. Levine was also president of Bradford College (1982–1989) and
senior fellow at the Carnegie Foundation for the Advancement of
Teaching and the Carnegie Council on Policy Studies in Higher
Education (1975–1982).

Jeanette S. Cureton currently divides her time between higher education research and Elmhurst College in Illinois, where her husband
is president. Prior to moving to the Chicago area in 1994, she served
as assistant to the president at Curry College in Milton, Massachusetts, and as a research assistant to Arthur Levine at the Harvard
Graduate School of Education. She is a Phi Beta Kappa graduate of
Bates College and holds an M.A.T. from Johns Hopkins University
and an Ed.M. from Harvard University.

   With Levine, Cureton has conducted research on the issue of
poverty and access to higher education, on multiculturalism and the
curriculum, and on college students of the 1990s. These studies have
led to workshops, presentations, and articles in *Change* magazine
and the *Review of Higher Education*. She also has engaged in research
on general education with the New England Resource Center for
Higher Education.

1

Generation Without a Name

It used to be that those of us who grew up in the '80s belonged to a generation without a name or even a press agent. But no longer. Ever since Time discovered the "twentysomething generation" in the summer of 1990, every major cultural institution—from Taco Bell to the Clinton campaign—has tried to devise a twentysomething contraption of its own.

> Alexander Star, "The Twentysomething Myth"

What really bothers me is my generation. When we are referred to as "Generation X" or the "lost generation," the media and the critics can get away with it, because we have failed to name ourselves through a purpose or a mission. As a friend of mine who is into cultural studies puts it, "It is the naming of the nameless." Maybe there is a mystical message in all of this. But politically, it's been devastating.

> Akiba Lerner, "My Generation"

Generation X is just a bunch of whiners, right? They're all slackers. They're all sleeping in their clothes, moaning about the national debt they've inherited, and pining for Greg or Marcia Brady.

> Come on. There are 38 million Americans in their
> 20s, but there are only two generalizations we can
> make about them with any degree of certainty: they
> are Americans, and they are in their 20s.
>
> Jeff Giles, "Generalizations X"

> You called us slackers. You dismissed us as Generation
> X. Well, move over. We're not what you thought.
>
> Time

Naming generations is something we like to do in the United States. However, "generation" is a rather slippery term and tends to be defined in two different ways. One is chronological, the group of people born at a common moment in time. The second is experiential, the group of people who live through common momentous events, including wars, political reigns, technological advances, disasters, and economic shifts. There is a good deal of overlap in the two definitions, though the second obviously includes a broad range of age groups.

This book uses both approaches. For the most part, it is a volume about a chronologically defined group of young people born in the 1970s and early 1980s who have attended college in the mid-to-late 1990s. However, periodically the focus shifts to the experiential to include all of the students attending college during the mid-to-late nineties regardless of age. These shifts of reference are noted in the text.

No matter which definition is used, there is a preoccupation in this country for searching out the distinctive characteristics in every new generation of young people, the ways in which the current generation seems different from the last. We then apply an appropriate sobriquet that somehow captures the salient features of the age. It is remarkably similar to how dogs get names like Blackie, Frisky, or Spot.

Every generation of young people since World War I has been so memorialized. The youth of the 1920s, stamped into history wearing raccoon coats, drinking from hip flasks, and dancing the Charleston, were anointed the "lost" generation. A decade later, young people who were out of work and out of luck were christened the "Depression" generation—in every sense of the term. The post-World War II youngsters, viewed as having donned gray flannel suits and hurrying to rebuild lives interrupted by the war, were named the "silent" generation. Then came the "baby boomers" of the 1960s, the generation of "sex, drugs, and rock and roll," forever remembered demonstrating in bell bottoms, love beads, and tie-dyed T-shirts. The late seventies and eighties produced what is now thought of as clones of the Michael J. Fox television character Alex Keaton from "Family Ties." They were conservative and conformist young people—well coifed, well dressed, and striving to be well-off. They were called the "me" generation.

The 1990s signaled arrival of a new decade and a new crop of young people. With them came a media barrage aimed at naming that generation. Who would be first to coin a name? Which name would stick? Who would get the credit? *Time* was the leader with a 1990 cover story, but major articles followed in magazines such as *Atlantic Monthly, U.S. News and World Report, Fortune, Business Week, New Republic,* and again in *Time* (Gross and Scott, 1990; Howe and Strauss, 1992; Saltzman, 1993; Deutschman, 1992; Zinn, 1992; Star, 1993; Hornblower, 1997). Books appeared with titles such as *Generation X* and *13th Gen* (Coupland, 1991; Howe and Strauss, 1993). Motion pictures included *Heathers, Singles, Pump Up the Volume, Slackers, Clueless,* and *Reality Bites.* There were television series, too: "Beverly Hills 90210," "Class of '96," and "Boston Common." Then came comic books, TV movies based on comic books, musical theater based on TV, and movies based on plays based on TV.

This media outpouring produced an impressive array of potential names for today's young people, rooted in all sorts of salient generational characteristics. The first of these names, "twentysomethings," focused on their age. Then came a grander notion based on their place in American history: the "thirteenth generation," or, more colloquially, "thirteeners." Demographics also provided a rationale for naming. The small size of the generation gave birth to "baby busters," or the even more popular "busters." Their perceived cultural tastes were celebrated in the name "MTV Generation" (after Music Television). Their personality traits—depending on whether one liked them or not—yielded "slackers" or, alternatively, "the repair generation," the former stressing social disengagement and the latter emphasizing social involvement.

There were directional names: the "upbeat" and the "downwardly mobile" generation. "Late bloomers" suggested an extended adolescence and sense of delayed realization of potential. Copycat names like the "lost" generation reflected a circular notion of generational history. There was a "we don't have a clue" name—"Generation X"—and a "we have only a small clue" name— "Posties." This was short for post-yuppies, meaning we were not quite sure who this generation is, but since they came after the yuppies ("young urban professionals"), we could be sure they were not that. This actually seems a variation on the place-in-history approach to naming.

Another familiar approach was reflected in the name "generation Y," sometimes written as "generation why"—since they don't want to be generation X, they must be Y. Who knows why? Finally, completely forsaking any independent identity comes generation "neXt," a term that manages to convey little more than sequence and irony based on an inside joke.

Despite the incredible panoply of choices, the name that stuck was, of course, "Generation X," and the credit went to Douglas Coupland. But by 1995, he was not so sure he wanted the credit or even the name: "Now I'm here to say that X is over. I'd like to declare a moratorium on all the noise, because the notion that there now exists a different generation—X, Y, K, whatever—is no longer debatable. Kurt Cobain's in heaven, *Slacker*'s at Blockbuster, and the media refers to anyone aged 13 to 39 as Xers" (Coupland, 1995, p. 72).

With all this noise then, what name makes the most sense for this generation? The choices are impressive, varied, and even contradictory. None seems exactly right. The most common, with its implications of anonymity, is "Generation X," or, as it has been shortened, "Xers." Only one in ten young people would use the phrase to describe themselves and, as the rapper Dr. Dre was quoted as saying, "I haven't heard anyone in my 'hood talking about it. The only X I know is Malcolm X" (Giles, 1994, p. 64). One of the earliest names for this generation, "twentysomethings," is still used regularly, but there is even less affinity for this term by its designees. *Newsweek* commented, "It makes it sound like everyone will get kicked out of the club when they get too old. Is this a generation or is it Menudo?" (Giles, 1994, p. 64)

Even more confusing than these names have been the generational portraits in which they have appeared. *Fortune* magazine, in an article titled "The Upbeat Generation," described today's young people as optimistic about their personal future, with expectations of doing as well as their parents. They were satisfied with their career prospects and rejected the claims of the "me" generation, despite being pessimistic about the future of the country. Instead, they were committed to living interesting lives, in which the personal took precedence over a job. Marriage was an essential; almost nine out of ten expected to marry only once. They saw education as a path to personal growth as well as money (Deutschman, 1992). Five years later, *Time* magazine published an almost identical account (Hornblower, 1997).

In contrast, the same youngsters were described as shut out, angry, neglected, and pessimistic about their personal futures in a *Business Week* article titled "Move Over, Boomers: The Busters are Here—and They're Angry." Young people were said to be destined for "mundane and marginally challenging work that provides a paycheck and little else" (Zinn, 1992, p. 76). They were more likely than past generations to be unemployed, underemployed, and living at home after completing school. This was a generation that resented the baby boomers for blocking their career paths. Not only were they economically at risk, but their world was emotionally unstable. They shared little in common beyond a collective sense of foreboding as they faced AIDS, crumbling families, and a sinking economy. The movies *Reality Bites* and *Slackers* presented the same picture.

After reading these accounts and viewing these films, one is forced to conclude either that this is a Jekyll-and-Hyde kind of generation, careening between optimism and pessimism, satisfaction and despair, or, alternatively, that we have not quite pinned down who these young people are.

There is probably some truth in both conclusions. The images we have formed of past generations of young people are caricatures. For example, the commonly held image of the youngsters of the sixties bears little resemblance to reality. In the main, 1960s youth were not political. In 1969, near the height of the sixties' youth protest, less than a third of all undergraduates (28 percent) had participated in a demonstration (Gallup International, 1969). In 1970, during the week of the most widespread campus unrest in U.S. history following the shooting of students at Kent and Jackson state universities, 43 percent of the nation's colleges and universities were entirely unaffected (Peterson and Bilurosky, 1971). Moreover, student political attitudes in the sixties remained middle-of-the-road or conservative; only a third of the undergraduates in 1969 described themselves as liberal or left of center (Undergraduate Survey, 1969). Most students (59 percent) came to college in 1969 for the same reasons students always had: to get training and skills for an occupation (Undergraduate Survey, 1969). One-half (49 percent) saw the chief benefit of a college education as increasing their earning power (Undergraduate Survey, 1969).

The generational images that we form grow out of the continuing shifts and changes in the attitudes, values, and behaviors of young people. For the most part, these shifts represent changes in degree rather than kind; nonetheless, they capture the nation's interest. We use them to define and label generations, and with time the labels become more real than the generations themselves. They evolve into stereotypes and cartoons, which eclipse the great diversity that exists within every generation. This is what happened with our image of the young people of the 1960s and each generation before and after them.

More and more, portrayals of this new generation seem to recognize the contradiction inherent in trying to name it. In attempting a summary, the trade journal *Brandweek* called them "a complex mix of contrasts" (Benezra, 1995, p. 34). One book (Holtz, 1995) declared on its jacket that "a media sound bite does not make a generation; demographics, politics, culture, and economics do." Another, titled *Generation Ecch!* (Cohen and Krugman, 1994), simply mocked it all and stated, "No more stinking labels!"

The popular characterizations of this generation that have surfaced over the decade are both accurate and inaccurate. Each attempts to capture some particular aspect, but none adequately describe the generation as a whole. While a full appreciation of such a complex group and its place in history will require the perspective of time, we can enlarge our understanding today with systematic research. This book seeks to present a portrait of a special slice of the generation, the young people most likely to lead the nation and the generation itself: today's college students.

The Life and Times of Today's College Students

Most of today's college freshmen of traditional age, the students who will be graduating in the year 2001, were born in 1979. This means they were born a decade and a half after John Kennedy's "New Frontier" ended and Lyndon Johnson's "Great Society" began. They were born after Martin Luther King Jr. and Robert Kennedy died. They were born after astronauts landed on the moon. They were born after Watergate and Richard Nixon's resignation, after the war in Vietnam, after Jimmy Carter was elected president, Apple Computer came into existence, the Concorde airplane took flight, and Anwar Sadat and Menachem Begin signed the Camp David Accord.

The towering figures in the lives of older adults are not part of their lives. More than four out of ten of today's undergraduates have never heard of Hubert Humphrey (42 percent) and Gloria Steinem (45 percent). Almost one-half (48 percent) do not recognize the names Barry Goldwater and Ralph Nader (Undergraduate Survey, 1993).

The events that stand out in the lives of older adults are not part of the lives of current college students either. These events do not summon the same emotions—sadness, anger, happiness, or hope—in them that they do for us. These events are at best history for current undergraduates.

They have lived their lives in a different era. Traditional-age students of the class of 2001 were born the year Americans were taken hostage in Iran, a nuclear accident occurred at Three Mile Island, and the federal government bailed out the Chrysler Corporation. They were one year old when Ronald Reagan won a landslide presidential election and John Lennon was shot. They were two when AIDS was identified, MTV made its debut, and the first U.S. software patent was issued. They were three when unemployment hit its highest level in the United States since the Depression; the Equal Rights Amendment failed to be ratified; and, for the first time, a majority of their mothers were employed outside the home. They were four when the compact disc was first sold and Sally Ride became the first U.S. woman in space. They were five when the Bell telephone system was broken up.

They were six when Gorbachev came to power in 1985, America became the leading debtor nation in the world, and the United States invaded Grenada. They were seven when the *Challenger* exploded, the Chernobyl nuclear accident occurred, the United States bombed Libya for terrorist acts, and Wall Streeter Ivan Boesky paid a $100 million criminal fine. They were eight when the *intifada* began in Palestine, the stock market crashed, and Oliver North testified before Congress in the Iran-Contra hearings. They were nine when George Bush was elected to the presidency. They were ten when the Berlin Wall came down, China killed thousands of pro-democracy demonstrators in Tiananmen Square, the *Exxon Valdez* spilled eleven million gallons of oil into Prince William Sound, and the U.S. government rescued the savings and loan industry.

They were eleven when America fought a war in the Persian Gulf, Nelson Mandela was released, and the two Germanies became one. They were twelve when the Soviet Union broke apart, apartheid laws were repealed in South Africa, and Clarence Thomas was elevated to the Supreme Court. They were thirteen when Bill Clinton was elected the forty-second president of the United States, three hundred current and former members of Congress were named in the House of Representatives banking scandal, U.S. troops were sent to Somalia, riots broke out in Los Angeles following the Rodney King verdict, and wars of ethnic cleansing began in Bosnia-Hercegovina. They were fourteen when Itzhak Rabin and Yasser Arafat shook hands after signing the Israeli-Palestinian peace accord, the Branch Davidian stand-off with federal agents occurred in Waco, Texas, and twelve western European nations created the European Community. They were fifteen when the World Series was canceled because of a major league players' strike and rock musician Kurt Cobain committed suicide. They were sixteen when Newt Gingrich became Speaker of the House of Representatives, O. J. Simpson was acquitted in his criminal trial, and a terrorist explosion destroyed the federal building in Oklahoma City. They were seventeen when the prime minister of Israel was assassinated, the Unabomber suspect was arrested, and Bill Clinton was reelected to office. They were eighteen when Simpson was found guilty at his civil trial, when the Dow Jones industrial average, continuing its unprecedented upward swing, topped 8,000 for the first time, and when Diana, Princess of Wales, died tragically in an automobile accident in Paris.

The picture that emerges is of a generation of young people living in a time of profound change—demographic, economic, technological, global, and social. Demographically, their numbers are smaller than any generation in recent memory. In 1970, fifteen-to-nineteen-year-olds made up nearly 10 percent of the population. By 1995, the proportion had declined by more than a quarter, to just 6.9 percent (U.S. Department of Commerce, 1996). As a result, current undergraduates grew up little noticed and overshadowed by the largest birth cohort in American history, the baby boomers.

However, the population decline was not uniform. During the 1980s and early 1990s, the number of fifteen-to-nineteen-year-old Caucasians dropped by 19 percent. Blacks of those ages decreased by 6 percent, resulting in a proportional population increase relative to whites. American Indians increased by 18 percent, and Hispanics grew by 42 percent. Asian Americans rose by over 100 percent (U.S. Department of Commerce, 1996). The net effect was a sharp rise in the proportion of teenagers of color. As a consequence, today's college students are members of the most racially diverse generation in U.S. history. From their earliest days, they have lived in a world in which the politics of race and ethnicity looms large. In this sense, their experience was dramatically different from that of their parents and the older adults around them, who were no better able to respond to these new conditions than they were and had less pressure to do so.

Economically, they were born in the last quarter of what Henry Luce termed "the American Century." It was a time in which U.S. economic supremacy waned. Trade balances with the rest of the world declined in key industries, such as automobiles, consumer electronics, machine tools, semiconductors, computers, copiers, textiles, and steel (Kennedy, 1993). Between 1975 and 1994, the U.S. trade balance went from a surplus of a little over $9 billion to a deficit of almost $150 billion (U.S. Department of Commerce, 1996).

Over the same period, the national debt ballooned nearly tenfold, from $533 billion in 1975 to almost $5 trillion in 1995 (U.S. Department of Commerce, 1996). The consequence was that interest payments increased from 9.8 percent of the national budget in 1975 to 22 percent in 1995 (*World Almanac and Book of Facts*,

1997). The dollar moved in the opposite direction. Between 1975 and 1995, its purchasing power declined nearly two-thirds (*Universal Almanac*, 1997). In this environment, consumer prices soared. The cost of a home more than tripled between 1975 and 1995, increasing from $42,000 to $159,000 for a one-family house (*Universal Almanac*, 1997). Poverty rates reflected the changes. Between 1975 and 1994, the number of Americans living below the poverty line increased nearly 50 percent (U.S. Department of Commerce, 1996). The term "homelessness" entered the *Encyclopaedia Britannica* in 1986.

The bottom line for today's traditional-age college students is that they grew up in a time when the nation's economic condition worsened. Although such leading indicators as lower unemployment rates, a bullish stock market, and record-breaking Dow Jones highs have more recently pointed to a healthier economy, for college students the gains were offset by broadscale personnel layoffs, warnings by the Federal Reserve chairman of hyperinflation on Wall Street, and the continuing flight of jobs to other countries. Scandals on Wall Street and in the banking industry regularly filled newspapers and television screens. Foreign investors bought well-known U.S. corporations—and even landmarks. A cornucopia of books was published on why the United States was uncompetitive internationally, and it was charged repeatedly, as the national debt rose, that the country was robbing tomorrow to pay for today.

It was an environment that caused young people to worry ceaselessly about their futures. Would there be "good" jobs for them? Would they have any economic security? Would they ever be able to afford a home and a family? Would they live in a country in which economic prospects were continuously declining?

Current undergraduates came of age with the opening of a new era. Within the space of a century, the United States had moved from an agricultural to an industrial base and toward a new kind of economy that highlighted service, information, and technology. While current students were growing up, the agricultural sector of the economy continued to contract. The number of farms in the country decreased by 15 percent between 1980 and 1995 (U.S. Department of Commerce, 1996). Manufacturing jobs dropped by 10 percent (U.S. Department of Commerce, 1996), and the number of workers in labor unions fell by over 40 percent (*World Almanac and Book of Facts*, 1997). This was accompanied by a boom in service industry jobs, which more than doubled between 1980 and 1995 (U.S. Department of Commerce, 1996).

Along with the job increase came a raft of new technologies: personal computers, software, genetic engineering, space shuttles, fiber optics, CD-ROMs, and digital audio tape. The inventions moved quickly from the laboratory to the home. Videocassette recorders were developed two years before the current freshmen were born; by 1995, VCRs were in 85 percent of all American homes (*Universal Almanac*, 1997). In the same year, more than 65 percent of households had cable television (*Universal Almanac*, 1997) and over 80 percent had microwave ovens (*World Almanac and Book of Facts*, 1997). In 1995 alone, almost 18 million answering machines were sold, 6 million cellular phones, and 8.4 million computers (*Universal Almanac*, 1997). Compact discs, which came to the U.S. marketplace in 1983, when the current freshmen were four, were the most popular format for music less than ten years later. Today, two-thirds of all music is sold on CD (*Universal Almanac*, 1997). The World Wide Web, created in 1989 when today's freshmen were ten, now reaches well over 25 million people and is growing exponentially (*Universal Almanac*, 1997).

Intermixed with these technological successes were failures of stunning magnitude. A 1984 Union Carbide chemical leak in Bhopal, India, killed 2,000 and injured 150,000 more. Nuclear accidents in the United States and Russia rocked the world. The largest oil spill in history emptied millions of gallons of crude oil into Alaska's Prince William Sound. A space shuttle explosion killed a crew of seven while the world watched on television. The U.S. Navy cruiser *Vincennes* accidentally shot down an Iranian passenger jet. The Hubble telescope was launched with a faulty mirror. Scientists reported that spray cans utilizing chlorofluorocarbons were destroying the earth's ozone layer.

In short, current undergraduates grew up during a period of history that will undoubtedly be called a technological revolution (for good or ill). During their childhood, communications were transformed in the United States thanks to computers, fax machines, e-mail, VCRs, cellular telephones, fiber optics, CDs, cable, phone mail, the World Wide Web, and more. But it was a quiet revolution, a few more appliances each year in the home, the school, and the office. Talk of science-fiction-like tomorrows seemed truly distant, with robots in the home, limitless energy sources, cryogenics, and commercial space travel. More real and immediate were the accidents and failings of technology, which were instantaneously transmitted by an expanding global media. Young people came to fear environmental catastrophe and technological disaster. Would the world in which they lived even be habitable? Would their lives be cut short by one or another impending cataclysm?

At least as tumultuous were the global changes—unification, atomization, alliances, civil collapse—that occurred while current undergraduates were growing up. Communism, the bogeyman of American society since World War II, fell seemingly overnight. Day after day in 1989, 1990, and 1991, the media broadcast reports of countries across central and eastern Europe turning away from Communist governments. One night the Berlin Wall came down; another day the Soviet Union banned the Communist party. Fifteen new nations were formed, while established countries—East Germany, Czechoslovakia, Yugoslavia, and the very Union of Soviet Socialist Republics—ceased to exist, with some of these regions lapsing into "ethnic cleansing" and civil wars.

In other parts of the world, old enemies came together: Israelis and Arabs, blacks and whites in South Africa. Western Europe formed a union. North America became a free trade zone. Still, the transformations and trends were dizzying, seemingly without order.

Former Communists returned to power in Poland. Skirmishes, threats and posturing continued between Israelis and Palestinians. Quebec threatened to secede from Canada. Students rebelled and were crushed in China. U.S. troops fought in Latin America, Africa, and the Middle East. Worldwide terrorism—bombings, kidnappings, and murders—struck seemingly everywhere: at airplanes, ships, automobiles, government buildings, places of worship, stores, workplaces, and homes on every continent. Nuclear weapons spread to North Korea, South Africa, the former Soviet states, and Iraq.

A new world order was being formed. The United States found its economic future inextricably interconnected with that of the rest of the world. American jobs, industries, financial markets, banks, material consumption, and the value of the dollar were determined as much by events abroad as at home. The Pacific Rim emerged as an economic power. Not just economically mighty Japan but, astonishingly for most Americans, South Korea, Taiwan, Singapore, and Hong Kong rose as world economic leaders.

For young people, the givens, the things older adults could once count on—a perpetual arms race, the Berlin wall, and apartheid in South Africa—simply no longer existed. The position of the United States in the world seemed less clear, and far less strong. Foreign policy became much more confusing as old justifications and standards lost their intuitive appeal. For Americans, new threats emerged and an uncertain future loomed on a shrinking globe. In their darkest moments, youngsters worried about living in a country sliding quickly into decline. Would they experience the equivalent of Rome or Greece after the fall?

Socially, the environment for youngsters changed too. The streets became more dangerous. Between 1978 and 1995, the number of forcible rapes rose by 45 percent, violent crime by 66 percent, and homicides by 10 percent (*World Almanac and Book of Facts,* 1997), despite substantial declines in the crime rates during the 1990s. In 1990 alone, firearms accounted for one-quarter of all deaths among fifteen-to-nineteen-year-olds (*Universal Almanac,*

1994). One in six youngsters between the ages of ten and seventeen had actually seen, or known, someone who had been shot (Adler, 1994). The nation's prison population reflected the increases. It more than tripled between 1980 and 1994 (*Universal Almanac*, 1997). The media, local and national, headlined the worst of the crime stories daily, making the growing violence seem even more pervasive than it actually was. Before completing elementary school, the average child would have watched eight thousand murders and one hundred thousand acts of violence on television (Adler, 1994).

This occurred at a time in which the social institutions that historically nurture the young were becoming less powerful. The family was a prime example. Between 1975 and 1992, the percentage of births to unmarried women more than doubled, from 14 percent to 30 percent (*Information Please Almanac*, 1996). More parents worked outside the home. The proportion of mothers in the labor force rose by 44 percent between 1975 and 1994—and they joined the workforce when their children were younger (*Information Please Almanac*, 1996). A rising percentage of youngsters lived in single parent families; by 1995, three out of every ten children lived with one or no parent (*Universal Almanac*, 1997). Childhood poverty increased by more than one-third during the 1970s and 1980s. In 1995, more than one in five youngsters were living below the poverty line (*World Almanac and Book of Facts*, 1997).

At the same time, the place of religion in the lives of young people diminished. Between 1976 and 1991, the proportion of high school seniors attending religious services weekly dropped by one-quarter (U.S. Department of Education, 1993). School activities also claimed a smaller portion of student lives. During the 1980s, student participation rates in high school extracurricular activities fell in athletics, cheerleading, hobby clubs, and vocational groups (U.S. Department of Education, 1996b; U.S. Department of Commerce, 1996).

The inescapable conclusion is that today's college students grew up in a time in which everything around them appeared to be changing—and often not for the better. They came of age in that environment without the traditional protection and cushion that the family, church, schools, and youth groups offered their predecessors. Looking at these realities, a 1994 issue of *Newsweek* concluded in its cover story that the "new fears and pressures [were] robbing a generation of its childhood." Our children were "growing up scared" (Adler, 1994, p. 43). A year later, *Time* reported that adolescents were "in danger of becoming lifelong casualties" of the problems they face as teenagers (Wulf, 1995, p. 86).

In 1819, Washington Irving wrote "Rip Van Winkle," a story about a man who fell asleep for twenty years. He awakened unaware of the length of his slumber and proceeded to walk around the village in which he lived. He found that "The very village was altered; it was larger and more populous. There were rows of houses which he had never seen before, and those which had been his familiar haunts had disappeared. Strange names were over the doors—strange faces at the windows—everything was strange" (Irving, [1819] 1961, p. 47). The same was true of the village populace. "The very character of the people seemed changed. There was a busy, bustling, disputatious tone to it, instead of the accustomed phlegm and drowsy tranquillity" (p. 48). Rip concluded: "Everything changed and I'm changed and I can't tell what's my name, or who I am" (p. 50).

Irving's story was an allegory. It was more than a tale of a man who overslept; it was an account of the relentlessness of change in America, a new nation with a shifting population, then in the early throes of an industrial revolution. Rip Van Winkle was intended to be everyman, trying to orient himself to an unfamiliar world that seemed to have changed radically overnight.

Today's college students grew up in a comparable time. As one observer put it, writing in *Newsweek*, "It wasn't until recently that I began to have some inkling of what poor Rip must have been feeling the day he finally opened his eyes and rejoined the world" (Janoff, 1995, p. 10). When asked in a survey at the University of

Colorado what adjective they would use to describe themselves, the most common choice was "tired."

The succeeding chapters portray a generation that is indeed wearied by the enormous pressures they face economically, politically, socially, and psychologically. At the same time, they are energized by a desire to enjoy the good life and make their corner of the world a better place. This is a generation in which hope and fear are colliding.

2

Flaws, Problems, and Decline
The New Localism

"I can't do anything about the theft of nuclear-grade weapons materials in Azerbaijan, but I can clean up the local pond, help tutor a troubled kid, or work in a homeless shelter."

Student, University of Colorado, Boulder

E very college generation is a product of its age. The momentous occurrences of its era—from the wars and economic shifts to the elections and inventions of its times—give meaning to the lives of the individuals who live through them. They also serve to knit those individuals together by creating a collective memory and a common historic or generational identity.

The Last Cold War Generation

We asked current undergraduates what social or political events most influenced their lives. We wanted to examine their attitudes, values, and beliefs, and how they came to hold them. We also wanted to learn how and why these beliefs differed from those held by students twenty or thirty years ago. Through surveys and interviews, we sought the answers to these and other questions.

Between 1992 and 1997 we undertook a series of studies of undergraduate student life on our nation's college and university campuses. Via written questionnaires we surveyed 270 student affairs officers at a representative sample of the nation's colleges and universities and nearly ten thousand undergraduates, also representative of the country. Daylong campus visits to twenty-eight diverse colleges and universities followed in the wake of the questionnaires. The schools we visited were public and private, religious and nonsectarian, residential and commuter, big and small, coeducational and single-sex, black and interracial, two-year and four-year colleges in every region of the country. During those visits, nearly fifty student affairs officers and three hundred students were interviewed, some individually and others in groups. In short, we sampled the opinions of traditional-age and nontraditional-age undergraduate students representing the scope of American higher education.

Two similar rounds of studies had been undertaken by the Carnegie Foundation in 1969 and again in the years 1976 through 1979. Throughout this book, we have used the earlier data to provide continuity and a comparison for our current findings. Details about these studies—what we've called the Undergraduate Surveys, Student Affairs Surveys, and the Campus Site Visits—can be found in Appendix A.

When we asked students about the social and political events that had had an impact on their lives, as an illustration we told them the children born after World War I might have answered, "the Great Depression." For those born a few years later, the response might have been the bombing of Pearl Harbor, World War II, or perhaps the death of Franklin Roosevelt. For the authors' generation, born shortly after the Second World War, the key event was the assassination of John Kennedy. People our age remember where they were when they heard the news; the whole world changed in its aftermath. When the same question was asked of undergraduates in the late 1970s and early 1980s, their most frequent answers were Vietnam and Watergate, followed by the civil rights movement and the assassination of national leaders during the 1960s.

On our 1993 Undergraduate Survey, today's college students gave six frequent answers to the question (Table 2.1). In interviews, they added a seventh.

The Gulf War was the most frequently cited event in students' lives. They described it as "our first war." "Every generation has a war; this was ours." When we first started interviewing students in 1992, they talked about their campus experiences, saying they watched the war on television. TVs in student lounges, which were usually turned to soap operas, stayed fixed on the war. As one student put it, "The TV in the Union was never on news before the war. Yeah; it was on 'American Gladiators' or 'Oprah' or soaps. But then everyone wanted to watch the war." With the rise of the Cable News Network (CNN), students joked that friends would drop by their rooms and say, "You want to watch the war for a while?" and off they would go.

Despite widespread fear among students of a renewed draft and another potential Vietnam, in 1993 undergraduates said the Gulf War pulled them together. It "brought back patriotism." Many knew people who had been called up to serve in the Gulf. On their

Table 2.1. Social and political events rated by undergraduates as key or very significant: 1993.

Social and political events	Percentage rating as significant
Persian Gulf War	89
Challenger explosion	84
Fall of Berlin Wall	84
Exxon Valdez oil spill	84
Rodney King affair	83
Breakup of the USSR	81
AIDS	[a]

[a]This item was not included in the student survey. It was mentioned, however, in every focus group interview with students.

Source: Undergraduate Survey (1993); Campus Site Visits (1993).

campuses, demonstrations opposing the war tended to be tiny or nonexistent in comparison with those in favor. Flags and yellow ribbons appeared in profusion. The initial student reaction was pride: "We're still number one"; the United States "can get things done." This was generally true among both liberal and conservative students.

In the years since, undergraduate reactions have changed. Current students are much more critical:

"It's still a mess."

"We didn't finish the job."

"It didn't accomplish anything."

"We botched another one."

"We were not told the truth."

"It made the situation worse."

"No reason to be there."

"Only a political show."

"Government is corrupt."

"Bush just wanted to be a hero."

"Men were risking their lives and then had to return and not get jobs."

"We were there to keep our oil prices down."

"Did it for economic interests only."

"People with money run the country."

Another reaction today is, "I don't remember the war that well."

Today, few students are willing to speak out in favor of the Gulf War or offer noneconomic rationales for it. In conversation after

conversation, students disavowed the U.S. role as world peace officer. They rejected the notion that "when anything goes wrong, we
have to straighten it out."

Their second most frequently mentioned event was the *Challenger* explosion. Once a student mentioned it in any group interview, the other student members of the group commonly nodded in
affirmation or said "yes." It was the equivalent of the Kennedy assassination for older adults. The students all knew where they were
when they heard the news. Many watched it on television in school;
the others saw it "on the news over and over and over again." They
often reported that they had been scheduled to have one of the
astronauts, Christa McAuliffe, teach them from space. For a number, it was the first time they had ever seen an adult (their own
teacher) break down and cry. It was for many their first brush with
death.

That students gave as an answer the *Challenger* explosion sur-
prised us. The space shuttle disaster was not on our original list of
responses we thought students might give to our question. Our generation had witnessed other fatalities in the space program; the
Challenger explosion was a very sad event, but it did not seem to us
to be a defining moment for the nation.

We asked the students why they had selected the *Challenger*.
Beyond the fact that it was their first shared generational tragedy,
they talked of a shattering of both their idealism and their sense of
safety:

"We lost our innocence."

"I always thought NASA was perfect."

"There were smashed dreams because of it."

"My hopes were in it. There was an Asian, a black,
    and a woman."

"Thought America was invincible."

"It was a national embarrassment."

"Burst my bubble."

"It was something good and then it blew up."

"NASA fell off its pedestal."

"Indicative of government corruption."

"Symbolizes whole era of the eighties—a big charade . . .
pulled the wool over our eyes."

Students also said the *Challenger* explosion was a "wake-up call"
or "reality check" for them and the nation. For some, it was "a sign
of a lot of things wrong" with the United States, such as government and manufacturing; for others, it highlighted the decline of
America, the nation's inability to compete economically and technologically. As one student put it, until then "I thought we were
the best; we're really only second class."

The fall of Soviet communism was another event students cited.
They spoke in terms of "pride," "hope," "drama," "energy," and "a
closer world." "We won the cold war." The symbol of communism's
fall that stood out most vividly for students was the razing of the
Berlin Wall, even more so than the dismemberment of the Soviet
Union. Again and again, students said, "I always thought the Berlin
Wall would never come down."

Today's undergraduates are the last cold war generation. They
studied Russia in school: "It was always the enemy." Although none
of the traditional-age undergraduates saw Khrushchev bang his shoe
on a table at the United Nations or lived through the Cuban mis-
sile crisis, many had seen films like *The Day After* and *War Games*,
which warned of the danger of nuclear war. A small number of students mentioned President Reagan's reference to the Soviet Union
as the "evil empire." They talked of seeing the ever-present "big
black bag" carried by the president. As a group, the students interviewed were afraid of the Soviet Union and afraid of the prospect

of nuclear holocaust. So the fall of communism was greeted by undergraduates as a very positive event.

However, they were quite somber about the consequences. Current students talk regularly about the instability of central and eastern Europe, of a tottering Russia. They fear Vietnam-like ground wars in places such as Bosnia. They noted almost as frequently the danger of a now-uncontrolled ex-Soviet nuclear arsenal. They often wondered whether the world was, in retrospect, a better place because of the demise of Soviet communism. Reflecting on this situation, one undergraduate said, "That is the way it's been for my generation. Every silver lining brings a cloud."

The *Exxon Valdez* was a very large cloud for students. Few undergraduates expressed surprise that the oil leak occurred. Rather, they believed there were little *Exxon Valdez*es every day: "It fits with Chernobyl, Three Mile Island, and the destruction of the Amazon rain forest." "We've been committing environmental suicide for centuries; we're making the world unlivable." They remembered seeing the oil spill on television day after day for months. What stood out for them was the extent of the damage and the long-term consequences; Prince William Sound "is never going to be the same again." Students blamed government and corporations for the oil spill, saying, "They don't care," "They are all corrupt," "Government always lies," and "Business only cares about making a buck."

There was a sense among students that the future was going to bring many more environmental accidents. In fact, undergraduates expressed greater fear of environmental pollution than they did of nuclear war. In one group interview, a student described the environment as "our generation's Vietnam." All of the members of the group agreed with her.

One more event students mentioned often was the Rodney King trial and the rioting that followed the verdict. Minorities—blacks, Hispanics, and Asian Americans—cited it most frequently but by no means exclusively. Students expressed polar opinions. Some were appalled by the initial verdict of not guilty for the police officers charged with using excessive force; others were repulsed by the subsequent violence. The only commonality was the strong negative reaction:

"I lost faith in the police."

"I lost confidence in people."

"It was a lesson in how to buy off a jury."

"Everything is politics."

"I used to believe the civil rights movement made a difference."

"Racism lives."

"Just because I don't hear the 'N' word any more doesn't mean it's gone."

"Laws were created, but minds were not changed."

"Another shock to the system."

"Rioting inexcusable."

"Lawless."

"Verdict really disturbed me."

"I was glad. It's the only way to get people to see."

"It reminded me that society treats me differently."

"Police jobs are stressful."

"What happened to King happened to everyone."

In group interviews, students added one item to the list of critical events in their lives: the AIDS epidemic, which had not been included in the undergraduate survey. AIDS has been a fact of life for this generation as long as sexual activity has been a possibility for them. Repeatedly, students said, "We grew up with it." Many reported being subjected to lectures, pamphlets, films, sermons, and condom demonstrations in school. They are "always throwing condoms at you." A common lament was, "I hear about it all the time. I'm tired of it." They were also often angry. They frequently compared their situation with that of the baby boomers, complaining that "when the baby boomers had sex, they got laid. When we have sex, we get AIDS." As one student said, "Free love is now more expensive."

Nonetheless, even though undergraduates resented this sword of Damocles hanging over their heads, the students interviewed felt AIDS could not happen to them. They felt immortal. Only a small minority of students knew anyone who had been diagnosed as HIV-positive.

What stands out in the seven events the students selected is the lack of one or two overpowering or dominant historical occurrences in the lives of current undergraduates. In contrast to the students of the late seventies and eighties who chose two principal events, Vietnam and Watergate, current undergraduates selected many different events. The student body president of Emerson College described the situation this way: "Our generation hasn't had any defining moment to really galvanize us. The hundred-day Gulf War wasn't enough to do that. We didn't have the Vietnam War. . . . We don't have a shared identity. There isn't anything holding us together or moving us."

Yet there is a common character to the events current students chose. They were all, at least in part, negative. Four of them—the *Challenger* explosion, the Rodney King affair, the *Exxon Valdez* accident, and AIDS—were described in wholly negative terms. The other three—the Gulf War and the fall of communism and of the Berlin Wall—also had negative consequences for students, particularly for our youngest undergraduates. In general, students thought they were living in a deeply troubled nation in which intractable problems were multiplying and solutions were growing more distant. They expressed the situation this way:

"Our experience is of flaws, problems, decline. We're not number one in anything. Our generation grew up with that."

"The world seems to be falling apart."

"We don't have anything that stable to hold onto."

"Rome and Greece fell; so can the U.S."

Social and Political Consequences

Current students have little confidence in the nation's social institutions, which they believe are deteriorating. Eight out of ten undergraduates said that business is too concerned with making profits and not concerned enough with public responsibility, the media is biased, Congress does not have the interests of the people at heart, the family is breaking down, and most people look out only for themselves. A majority of undergraduates also concluded that political leaders lack integrity, doctors are more motivated by money than by helping people, and most people will take advantage of you if they can (Table 2.2).

Undergraduates reserved their strongest criticism for government and the American political system. They don't believe either works. A majority of college students said meaningful social change cannot be achieved through traditional American politics. An even higher proportion of students, almost four out of five, stated that the political system is not working well at handling the country's problems (Undergraduate Survey, 1993). At Boston College, we met with a group of about one hundred student leaders. We asked how many of them believed the U.S. government could play a major part in solving the nation's problems. Six students raised their hands. The conversations that followed mirrored those of focus groups on

Table 2.2. Student attitudes regarding social institutions: 1993.

Attitudes toward social institutions	Percentage agreeing
Family values are breaking down in America.	83
Most people only look out for themselves.	82
Newspaper and TV journalists provide biased accounts of news events.	82
Private corporations are too concerned with profits and not enough with public responsibility.	81
Most people will take advantage of you if they can.	68
Doctors today are more motivated by money than by helping people.	63
In this country it is impossible for political leaders to maintain their integrity.	50
Most chief corporate executives deserve the high salaries they earn.	31
Congress has the interests of the people at heart.	21

Source: Undergraduate Survey (1993).

campuses across the country. Government and politics were viewed as the problem rather than the solution. In this respect, today's students were far more critical of politics, politicians, and government than their collegiate peers of past years (Table 2.3).

A Perverse Optimism

The irony is that students are remarkably upbeat about the future. Two out of three (66 percent) said they were optimistic about the future of the country (Undergraduate Survey, 1993). Their optimism was not the Pollyannaish variety traditionally associated with youth; this optimism had a hard edge. They gave answers such as "I expect things to get worse before they get better," "I'm pragmatically optimistic," and, our favorite, "I am cynically optimistic." This contrasts sharply with the students of the 1960s and 1970s. Two-thirds of the students (65 percent) surveyed in 1969 and 1976 stated

Table 2.3. Student attitudes regarding politics: 1969, 1976, 1993.

	Percentage agreeing		
Attitudes toward politics	1969	1976	1993
Meaningful social change cannot be achieved through traditional American politics.	50	44	57
Generally speaking our political system is working well in handling America's problems.	—	39	22

Source: Undergraduate Surveys (1969, 1976, 1993).

that they were "very apprehensive" about the nation's prospects (Undergraduate Surveys, 1969, 1976).

Hand in hand with this new optimism has come a rising sense of efficacy. Almost three out of four undergraduates (73 percent) believed that an individual can bring about change in our society. In the two prior surveys, nearly half of all students (45 percent) rejected this notion (Undergraduate Surveys, 1969, 1976, 1993).

When students were asked how they could be so negative about the country's social institutions (especially its government) and yet be so positive about its future and the possibilities for change, they gave a common answer (though with varying degrees of enthusiasm). It was always because of their generation:

"Our generation is getting more involved."

"The younger generation is more concerned with the planet."

"Our generation will be able to fix the problem."

"Our generation will do things."

"Our generation works hard. We will do something."

"We are the future. . . . Our generation cares about the country and society."

"Our generation will make a revolution."

"I'm like Mary Poppins. People have hope. Our generation can make a change. We are getting back to basics. We are recycling. There is a new, younger leadership."

The reality is that student political attitudes defy traditional labels. Undergraduates are both more liberal and more conservative than their predecessors of the past quarter century. Nearly two-fifths of undergraduates (38 percent) characterized themselves as liberals, and 28 percent called themselves conservatives. Since 1969, the political center has eroded for college students, in favor of the poles. In 1969, 44 percent of undergraduates said they were middle-of-the-road; that fell to 39 percent in 1976. Today the center stands at 29 percent (Undergraduate Surveys, 1969, 1976, 1993).

However, despite increasing polarization of student politics, undergraduates are not ideological. They do not fit into familiar political boxes. They oppose big government. A large majority favors term limits for elected officials, but nearly as many students want tougher environmental laws and almost one-half support busing to achieve racial integration. Undergraduates are fiscally conservative, but they do not want social programs cut and desire higher levels of government funding to combat AIDS. They are conservative on crime, favoring harsher criminal penalties while overwhelmingly supporting handgun control. They are liberal on abortion and conservative on drugs (Table 2.4). Current undergraduates are issue oriented, not ideological. They are concerned about a plethora of social problems and hold opinions, which range across the political spectrum, on how the nation should respond to those problems.

The fact of the matter is that students at ideological poles hold remarkably similar opinions. A majority of both liberals and conservatives favor congressional term limits, stronger environmental legislation, more government spending for AIDS, increased handgun controls, and a woman's right to choice. Similarly, they oppose reducing government spending on social programs, abolishing capital

Table 2.4. Student opinions on social issues, by political orientation: 1993.

Opinions on social issues	Percentage agreeing	
	Liberals	Conservatives
I support term limits for members of Congress.	81	88
I would support stronger legislation for the protection of the environment, even at the expense of economic growth.	81	58
Racial integration of public schools should be achieved even if it requires busing.	56	36
Taxes should be raised to reduce the federal deficit.	47	31
The United States is spending too much on social problems.	17	49
I favor government spending to combat AIDS.	90	63
There is too much concern in the courts with the rights of criminals.	62	82
Capital punishment should be abolished.	28	12
Laws should be enacted to control handgun sales and ownership.	86	65
A woman should have the freedom to choose whether or not to have an abortion.	91	54
Marijuana should be legalized.	42	19

Source: Undergraduate Survey (1993).

punishment, legalizing marijuana, and reducing the national debt by increasing taxes. Only on the issue of busing do conservatives and liberals diverge.

At the polls, these views translate into voting patterns that mirror the nation's. Among students registered to vote, 38 percent said they were enrolled in the Democratic party; 35 percent registered as Republicans; 1 percent belonged to other political parties; and the rest, 25 percent, were independents—precisely the same proportions as the rest of the country (Voter News Service, 1996).

Students cast their ballots like other Americans as well. In 1996, college-educated Americans (age eighteen to twenty-four) gave 50 percent of their votes to Clinton, 1 percentage point more than the country did; 34 percent to Dole, 7 percentage points less than the nation; and 9 percent to Perot, 1 percentage point more than the country (Voter News Service, 1996). In the 1992 presidential election, they gave 46 percent of their votes to Bill Clinton, 3 percentage points higher than the general electorate. Twenty percent voted for Ross Perot, 1 percentage point more than the rest of the country (Undergraduate Survey, 1993); and 33 percent cast their ballots for George Bush, 4 percentage points behind his national tally. This is in sharp contrast with 1988, when college students, like the rest of the country, overwhelmingly gave their votes to Republican George Bush over Democrat Michael Dukakis.

Desire for Change

The impact of students' distrusting government and being issue oriented rather than ideological became clear when they were asked why they voted the way they did. Rarely did students mention ideology; they seldom said such things as "I'm a Republican" or "I'm a liberal." Instead, the majority of undergraduates interviewed spoke of the need for change. Their most frequent explanation for how students vote was "Our generation wants change."

College students reject the nation's leaders. When given a list of twenty-six prominent Americans, the individuals whom undergraduates were most critical of were politicians. Topping their negative list were Ted Kennedy (66 percent), Richard Nixon (64 percent), Pat Buchanan (54 percent), Ronald Reagan (41 percent), George Bush (40 percent), and Jesse Jackson (37 percent) (Undergraduate Survey, 1993). The 1995 Student Leaders Survey had one addition, Newt Gingrich, who weighed in even more negatively than Ted Kennedy, at 67 percent. Interestingly, however, students were still withholding judgment in their evaluation of Bill Clinton. In toto, the people they rated so negatively were individuals whose politics run the gamut from very liberal to very conservative. The only thing these public figures have in common is that they are established career politicians. Also, it is remarkable that Jesse Jackson managed to make the transition so quickly in students' minds from protester to professional politico.

In contrast, the people students felt most positive about were outsiders. They were self-made people with a social agenda, who struggled against adversity and had reputations as populists (deserved or not). They included Margaret Thatcher (88 percent positive), Magic Johnson (78 percent), Nelson Mandela (78 percent), Boris Yeltsin (78 percent), Ross Perot (76 percent), and Lee Iacocca (76 percent) (Undergraduate Survey, 1993). None of the Americans on the list was a career politician. All of the politicians on the list were foreign, living far enough away to remain attractive. It is difficult to imagine a more ideologically heterogeneous group. What Nelson Mandela and Margaret Thatcher have in common politically could not fill a thimble, yet a majority of undergraduates gave positive ratings to both. This is indeed a postideological generation.

The postideological conclusion was also apparent in student attitudes in regard to the 1996 presidential election. On 78 percent of the nation's campuses, deans of students reported that undergraduates were not highly interested in the election (Student Affairs Survey, 1997). On 82 percent of college campuses, student interest was rated the same as or even lower than in 1992. Despite the efforts of college-based political parties and increased voter registration drives, the number of collegiate political events and campus visits by politicians was more likely to have declined than to have increased relative to 1992 (Table 2.5).

At bottom, college students live in a world in which they distrust the nation's leaders. They have no confidence in the country's social institutions. They see large social problems all around them, from poverty, racism, and crime to environmental pollution, a troubled economy, and global conflict. In their words, "Everything is wrong."

Despite their optimism about the future of America, as a generation students feel isolated and alone. They believe they are being made to assume responsibility unfairly for a horrendous array of social problems, selfishly created by their elders. Unlike their predecessors of the 1980s, current students have concluded that they

Table 2.5. The 1996 political campaign.

	Percentage of campuses reporting activity		
Political activity or events	Increased	Remained the same	Decreased
Level of student interest in the 1996 election	18	57	25
Number of political candidates visiting campus	26	42	34
Number of political events on campus	22	49	29
Student participation in local campaigns	23	60	17
Voter registration efforts	69	24	9
General activity by Young Democrats and College Republicans	26	46	28

Source: Student Affairs Survey (1997).

do not have the luxury of turning away from these problems. "We can't just look out for ourselves like the yuppies did." From the point of view of today's undergraduates, the problems are too large and getting worse, threatening to overwhelm them. Our generation has to "fix everything." They deeply resent that responsibility, saying, "It's unfair. We didn't make the problems; we inherited them."

The New Localism

Students do not believe there can be quick fixes or universal solutions. They do not expect government to come to the rescue. Instead, they have chosen to become personally involved and to focus locally, on their community, their neighborhood, and their block. Their vision is small and pragmatic; they are attempting to accomplish what they see as manageable and possible—like the student who said, "I can't do anything about the theft of nuclear-grade weapons materials in Azerbaijan, but I can clean up the local pond, help tutor a troubled kid, or work at the homeless shelter."

In taking on these tasks, they have heroes to guide them, or so said 55 percent of students. For the most part, the people they named were not famous figures or household names. A majority of the students cited as heroes dad, mom, Jesus, other relatives, friends, or neighbors (Table 2.6).

This marks an important change. When students in the late 1970s and 1980s were asked who their heroes were, their most common answer was no one, followed by God as a distant second and then entertainers and athletes, varying by season of the year and region of the country (Campus Site Visits, 1979).

What is remarkable today is that heroes are once again alive and well for undergraduates. This is certainly consistent with the rising levels of student optimism about the future.

It is also important that the kind of people students see as heroes has changed, too. They are now local; two out of three students

Table 2.6. Student heroes: 1993.

Heroes	Percentage reporting
Parents	29
Religious figure (usually Jesus)	14
Relative, friend, or neighbor	12
Entertainer	6
Teacher or professor	5
Politician or government leader	5
Athlete	5
Scientist, researcher, or scholar	2
Author	2
Business leader	2
Military leader	1
Journalist or reporter	1
Clergy	1
Other	12

Source: Undergraduate Survey (1993).

chose someone they knew personally. Even the switch from God to Jesus is worthy of note. Instead of a deity, students selected a personal savior.

Students rejected the larger-than-life figures traditionally thought of as heroes. They described these people as "inaccessible" and "up on a pedestal." They have "no faults" and are "not real." "No one could be like them." They thought "all public personalities have feet of clay." Besides, as one student put it, "Politicians and movie stars don't touch me. I can't relate to politicians on a one-on-one basis." They were more comfortable with words like "mentor" and "role model" than hero. An undergraduate at the Illinois Institute of Technology caught the sentiments of his peers when he said, "I prefer people I look up to. I don't idolize them, but . . . I would like to be like them."

This was the rationale students gave for the heroes they selected. Typical of their responses were the following:

Reasons for Choosing Mother as Hero

"She's been my role model. She's a child welfare social worker and keeps doing it year after year without burnout."

"Because of the things she's been through. I credit her with making me who I am."

"She's always been there for me. . . . She taught me my values. In a way, my heroes are all black women who are deserted by their men and still struggle on."

Reasons for Choosing Father as Hero

"Has grown up in third-world poverty and has made a success of himself."

"Hard worker; tenacious, an example . . . can be happy, even [in] hard times . . . a survivor."

"Always looked up to him. He's a great guy."

Reasons for Choosing Jesus as Hero

"He helped me to be here, to wake up every morning, to feel good, and to be here for my three daughters and myself."

"He's the reason I am what I am today and what I'll be tomorrow."

"He is everything to me."

Beyond choosing local heroes, students have translated their local commitment into community service. Nearly two-thirds of all undergraduates are currently involved in volunteer activities. A majority of students at all types of institutions are participating in volunteerism, at two-year colleges, four-year colleges, and universities, and in every region of the country. It is a fact among older and younger students, residential and nonresidential undergraduates, full-time and part-time. There is little variation in participation rates by race or age; it does not even matter whether students work or not while going to school. They are involved in service in unprecedented numbers (Table 2.7). Indeed, during the 1990s, three-quarters of all colleges and universities reported increases in student participation in volunteer activities (Student Affairs Survey, 1997).

Table 2.7. Characteristics of students involved in service: 1993.

Student characteristics	Percentage participating
All undergraduates	64
At two-year colleges	59
At four-year colleges	67
At universities	68
Full-time undergraduates	65
Part-time undergraduates	59
Males	62
Females	66
Commuter students	58
Residential students	75
Caucasians	65
Blacks	65
Hispanics	61
Asian Americans	55
Students 25 or younger	65
Students over 25	63
Students working more than 20 hours weekly	61
Students working less than 20 hours weekly	68
Students not working	64
Students in the Northeast	61
Students in the Midwest	65
Students in the South	64
Students in the West	67

Source: Undergraduate Survey (1993).

Their activities are remarkably heterogeneous, reflecting the local rather than national character of today's volunteerism. You name it, students are doing it. The most popular activities are those that have historically attracted undergraduates: fundraising (including clothing and food drives), working with children, and activities with religious sponsorship. But they are also involved with charities, the environment, the elderly, hospitals, Habitat for Humanity, and the homeless. Beyond this, they participate in programs for the handicapped, the mentally retarded, those needing hospice care, election campaigns, and anything else one can imagine (Table 2.8).

One of the most visible examples of youthful commitment to a cause is the case of twenty-four-year-old Adam Werbach, a recent graduate of Brown University, whose efforts to preserve the environment have resulted in his election to the presidency of the Sierra Club. As a high school student in smog-plagued Los Angeles, he founded the Student Sierra Coalition and during his college years built it into a nationwide group of thirty thousand activists. Now,

Table 2.8. Undergraduate service activities: 1993.

Type of work	Percentage participating
Fundraising	27
Children	24
Religious sponsored organization	24
Charity organization	10
Environmental	9
Elderly	9
Hospital	7
Homeless/soup kitchen	7
Handicapped	6
Election campaign	6
Mentally handicapped	4
Other	20

Source: Undergraduate Survey (1993).

as the youngest president of the august 600,000-member club, he aims to reach out to Generation X, who will respond to the call, he believes, if the educational process is fun and if the focus is on environmental issues of local import (Hornblower, 1997).

When undergraduates were asked why they got involved in service activities, they stressed the social contribution, saying they got satisfaction from helping people (80 percent) and felt it their responsibility to correct societal problems (54 percent) (Serow, 1991). A student working at an AIDS center described her experience this way: "I really felt like I was doing something even when I was just cleaning up or whatever. It gave me hope; maybe one person can actually make a difference. I felt like what I was doing mattered, that maybe for one moment, I could help someone by delivering condoms or just by listening. . . ."

Her response was fairly typical of what students said in small group interviews. However, it was by no means universal. By way of contrast, a classmate said his experience at a homeless shelter left him feeling "lost," "dirty," and "guilty."

Nor was social service the only rationale students offered for getting involved in these activities. Many undergraduates acknowledged that initially they "were volunteered," as opposed to volunteering themselves, by course assignment or membership in a club with a compulsory service project (56 percent). Others remarked that service is a great way to meet new people (49 percent) and, with newly acquired job skills, also not a bad way to build a résumé (42 percent) (Serow, 1991). When asked why the numbers of students participating in service were so high, a student body president joked that "service is PC" (politically correct). At the moment, it is certainly faddish on the campuses we visited and the PC thing to do.

But it would be a mistake to underestimate the sincerity of the students involved. Three-quarters of all the nation's chief student affairs officers reported rises in student participation rates on their campuses (Student Affairs Survey, 1997). Most tellingly, this was true even at commuter schools, in which a majority of students worked long hours at jobs. At one such college, a majority of the undergraduates interviewed were engaged in volunteer projects even though there was neither a campus volunteer organization nor service placements. They found these projects themselves in the communities in which they lived, often through their church. Their participation was not a lark or merely the thing to do; it required commitment, sweat, and serious juggling.

This wave of involvement has not escaped the nation's leaders. In the spring of 1997, President Clinton called a summit on the topic in Philadelphia, hoping to expand volunteerism to an even broader scale. Chaired by General Colin Powell, the summit sought to mobilize an army of corporations and individuals to reach out to at-risk youths through tutoring, mentoring, and other service programs. The aim was to bring the public, private, and nonprofit sectors together in an unprecedented effort to "save" an estimated two million kids by the year 2000 (Alter, 1997; Bennet, 1997). It is not clear, however, whether young people will join this initiative or feel it an invasion of the solution they have embraced on their own to overcome the deficiencies of government and the profit-making sector.

A New Breed of Political Organization

Reflecting the politics of today's undergraduates, a new breed of student organization has come into being in recent years. These organizations are generationally rooted, issue oriented, high-tech, and locally focused. One of the more active is SEAC, the Student Environmental Action Coalition. Pronounced "seek," it proclaims as its rallying cry "Unity is our generation's only hope for saving the planet" (Student Environmental Action Coalition, 1993, p. 3).

SEAC grew out of a 1988 ad placed in the magazine *Greenpeace* by undergraduates at the University of North Carolina, who asked students interested in forming an environmental network to get together. The result was national headquarters in North Carolina, lobbying offices in California and Washington, D.C., seventeen regions connecting all fifty states, chapters on more than twenty-two hundred high school and college campuses, and an international coalition from sixty-five countries. There have been four national conferences, the largest of which attracted seventy-six hundred student activists and a list of "environmental stars," including Robert Redford, Helen Caldicott, Jesse Jackson, and César Chávez. For the past three years, SEAC has sponsored a "national gathering" for its members, called SEAC-o-topia. This annual back-to-nature camping excursion hosts an in-depth organizers' workshop, with sessions ranging from "Corporate Agenda and the University" to "The Oral History of Activism."

The focus of SEAC is on local activities, and each region—indeed, each chapter—has its own agenda. The national headquarters support this activity with publications ranging from videos, CDs, and full-length books to fact sheets, resource packets, and campaign guides. For the most part, these materials are very pragmatic, with such titles as "SEAC Organizing Guide," "Strategic Media: Designing a Public Interest Campaign," "How to Do Newsletters," "How to Start or Revive a Local Group," "EcoLinking: Everyone's Guide to On-Line Environmental Information," and "SEAC Fundraising Guide."

There is also a group of people known as SEAC trainers, who are designated consultants for the local chapters. Each trainer is a person to whom local chapters can turn for advice, to test new ideas, or to plan new projects. SEAC suggests that the trainer, a troubleshooter of sorts who travels around the country, is there to help local groups, "whether you're not sure how to do a press conference or no one showed up at your last meeting."

SEAC also has taken advantage of the Internet and the World Wide Web in providing information and resources for local organizers. There are thirty-one e-mail discussion lists sponsored by SEAC, which allow the different caucuses, interest groups, and regions themselves to communicate effectively and easily through the Internet. SEAC's home page on the Web contains a host of information on the background of various initiatives, a centralized contact list for all SEAC regions, connections to Web resources on the environment, and an extensive calendar of events on both regional and national scales. This electronic network fulfills the basic SEAC function of providing a mechanism by which local activists can connect with each other nationally.

Beyond offering assistance, SEAC prepares local environmental leaders. It offers regular weekend training institutes, enrolling thirty undergraduates each. Led by experienced student leaders, these programs focus on bread-and-butter issues such as recruiting new members, planning strategy, developing coalitions, doing actions, and fighting racism and sexism.

Gender and race issues are high on the SEAC agenda. There are national caucuses for women, people of color, and gays, which are also useful vehicles for recruiting members and expanding participation. As if all this were not enough, SEAC also sells mugs, T-shirts, and bumper stickers. Baseball caps can't be too long in coming.

Despite this cornucopia of services, the action in SEAC is decidedly at the local level. A recent issue of its monthly magazine *Threshold* had eight columns of densely packed regional activities: protests and picnics, field trips and festivals, legislative lobbying and landfill initiatives, barbecues and boycotts. The rest of the magazine is devoted to articles detailing regional environmental concerns, written by the activists involved. At the end of many articles is a box with the heading "What *You* Can Do," with contact organizations, sample letters to politicians, and suggestions for background reading. Throughout the magazine there is far more diversity of events and issues than any commonality. Indeed, the only common issue the SEAC national office has been pushing recently has been opposition to the environmental impact of International Monetary Fund and World Bank policies. All the rest is up to the regions, the states, and the individual campuses.

Another, very different, organization which makes use of a similar grassroots, nonideological approach is Rock the Vote. Created in

1990 by the music industry in response to Tipper Gore's campaign against sexually graphic and violent children's music, it focused initially on anticensorship issues but moved quickly into getting young people more involved in the political process. Rock the Vote bills itself as a nonprofit, nonpartisan organization that does not endorse candidates. "We're partisan to protecting the rights of kids, that's all," said Jeff Ayeroff, cochairman of Virgin Records America and one of the organization's leaders (Stewart, 1996, p. 11a).

Rock the Vote claims responsibility for drawing two million new young voters to the 1992 election, reversing a twenty-year trend of declining participation. (They did less well in getting out the vote in 1996, when participation rates by eighteen-to-twenty-four-year-olds plummeted.) Through a wide range of promotions, concerts, endorsements, and free media exposure, Rock the Vote made the argument that this generation could make a difference in the outcome of an election by using the power of their numbers at the ballot box. The organization trumpeted registration through sponsored concert tours involving Genesis, U2, John Mellencamp, and Guns n' Roses. They took out full-page ads in big-city newspapers signed by the hottest musical acts in the country. Registration materials were distributed at thousands of record retail stores and more than three thousand Taco Bells. A voter registration special was even broadcast on Fox Television. As Ayeroff said at the time, "If we've been accused of unplugging a generation, I bet we could plug 'em back in" (Gowen, 1993, p. 18).

During the 1992 campaign, Rock the Vote joined forces with MTV, an incredible combination since the latter reaches more than 60 percent of all American homes.

The influence of Rock the Vote was undeniable in the 1993 passage of the federal Motor Voter bill, designed to simplify voter registration policies. The organization asked people to let Washington know they supported the bill via a clip-out "Dear Senator" card on the back of the R.E.M. album Out of Time, one of the top-selling records in 1993. This tactic alone generated more than 150,000

cards of support to Congress (Holland, 1992). At the signing cere-
mony, President Clinton singled out the organization for its role in
promoting the bill (showing a Rock the Vote post card he signed during the presidential campaign) and held a photo opportunity on the
White House lawn with Rock the Vote heads Jeff Ayeroff and Patrick
Lippert (Stewart, 1996). A U.S. Senate Rules Committee staffer
described Rock the Vote this way: "They weren't what you would call
heavy hitters on the bill, you know, like the League of Women Voters
. . . but their efforts in demonstrating that voter registration on college campuses works and getting young people to write to their sen-
ators were influential and helpful" (Holland, 1992, p. 81).

Rock the Vote has taken advantage of the provisions of the
Motor Voter bill to make it easier to register to vote. They set up a
toll-free number for phone-in registration, and their Web page has
an online registration form. Rock the Vote has a registration booth
that travels with the MTV "Choose or Lose" bus tour. They had
partnerships with Youth Vote '96, Black Youth Vote '96, and Latino
Vote '96 to coordinate voter registration. The organization is continuing its strategy of distributing voter registration materials
through the venues that already attract young people: concerts,
record stores, and music magazines ("Youth-Vote Group . . . ,"
1996). Celebrity endorsements include stars from television's "Mel-
rose Place" and "ER," rapper Coolio, and the band Hootie and the
Blowfish, whose MTV video features Rosa Parks, a hero of the civil
rights movement, and propounds the theme that "one person can
make a difference" (Rock the Vote, 1996). Their efforts have resulted
in more than 850,000 new voters since 1993, half a million in 1996
alone (Rock the Vote, 1997).

Through identifying issues that are relevant to young people
today, Rock the Vote is encouraging those who register to become
informed. Says Ricki Seidman, a former Clinton staffer who has run
the organization since 1994, "We're trying to help educate the voters now. We're saying that it's not enough just to register to vote"
(Stewart, 1996, p. 11a). By means of its Web site, Rock the Vote

provides information on issues such as national service, education, antiviolence campaigns, the environment, the economy, and health care. It does not patronize constituents by assuming it knows what they think about these issues. But Rock the Vote does want to ensure that young people's concerns—whatever they may be—are addressed by politicians (Stewart, 1996).

The nation's established political parties have watched and listened to organizations like Rock the Vote and SEAC. They have redesigned their youth programs to reflect the same themes. For example, a recent College Republican mailer said:

We're the New Generation
13-ers
Generation X, the MTV generation
and the wave of the future.

The ad spoke of the diversity of the members of the Republican party; proposed a series of action issues, both liberal and conservative; and closed with a challenge:

Do Something
It's Your Future
It's Our Generation
Do Something New

A Democratic mailer was less generational, but it emphasized local issues such as flood relief, national service, health care, family leave, crime prevention, and campaign reform. They sent e-mail and had buttons and T-shirts saying "Fighting for Change," the party's rallying cry. This theme dominated the Democratic literature, making its focus at least as generational as the literature of the Republicans.

If today's students, then, are yearning for and demanding change, they are motivated principally by their loss of faith in the nation's leaders and its social institutions to do the job. Heirs to a world in need of repair, they are angry that the burden of fixing it has fallen on their shoulders. They are overwhelmed by the immensity of the task and by the global scale of the issues facing them. At the same time, they are buoyed by a relentless optimism born of the conviction that their generation has the capacity to make a difference. For students of the 1990s, this efficacy is achieved through social action in the community, with heroes acting as guides. It is also achieved through political action on campus.

3

• •

Campus Politics
Let the Buyer Beware!

"They push right up to the limit but don't cross the line."
Student affairs officer, University of California,
Santa Barbara

Perhaps the largest change in higher education in recent years is who the students are. Between 1980 and 1994, the lion's share of college enrollment growth came from students who might be described as nontraditional (U.S. Department of Education, 1996b). By 1994, 44 percent of all college students were over twenty-five years old (U.S. Department of Education, 1996b), 54 percent were working (U.S. Department of Education, 1996e), 55 percent were female, and 43 percent were attending part-time (U.S. Department of Education, 1996b). Fewer than one in six of all current undergraduates fits the traditional stereotype of the American college student attending full-time, being eighteen to twenty-two years of age, and living on campus (U.S. Department of Education, 1996b).

What this means is that higher education is not as central to the lives of many of today's undergraduates as it was to previous generations. Increasingly, it is just one of a multiplicity of activities in which they are engaged every day. For many, college is not even the most important of these activities; work and family often overshadow it.

A Consumer Mentality

As a consequence, older, part-time, and working students, especially those with children, often say they want a different type of relationship with their colleges from the one undergraduates have historically had. They prefer a relationship like those they already enjoy with their bank, the telephone company, and the supermarket.

Think about what you want from your bank. We (the authors) know what we want: an ATM on every corner. We want to know that, when we get to the ATM, there will be no line. We would like a parking spot right in front of the ATM. We want our checks deposited the moment they arrive at the bank, or perhaps the day before. And we want no mistakes in processing—unless they are in our favor. We also know what we do not want from our banks. We do not want them to provide us with softball leagues, religious counseling, or health services. We can arrange all of these things for ourselves and don't wish to pay extra fees for the bank to offer them.

Students are asking roughly the same thing from their colleges. They want their colleges nearby and operating at the hours most useful to them, preferably around the clock. They want convenience: easy, accessible parking (in the classroom would not be at all bad); no lines; and polite, helpful, and efficient staff service. They also want high-quality education but are eager for low costs. For the most part, they are very willing to comparison shop, placing a premium on time and money. They do not want to pay for activities and programs they do not use. In short, students are increasingly bringing to higher education exactly the same consumer expectations they have for every other commercial enterprise with which they deal. Their focus is on convenience, quality, service, and cost.

On campus, students sound exactly like consumers too. Deans of students regularly report that their students "act like customers": "I can't tell you how many times a week a student walks into my office and says, 'I'm paying $25,000 a year, and I am unhappy with. . . .'" Students aren't particularly shy about expressing the same sentiments: "We're paying all this money," "I'm paying their salaries," or "I'm the customer."

One dean of students said, "I wish I had a dollar for every student who threatens to sue me." Actually, this could be a fairly lucrative arrangement, as 40 percent of all colleges and universities surveyed reported an increase in threats of litigation during the 1990s. One-half said threats had remained constant, and only 9 percent indicated declines (Student Affairs Survey, 1997). Fortunately, just a small proportion of the threats are actually translated into action, but the effect on institutions has been chilling; colleges think increasingly like businesses and are encouraged to treat students more like customers than family members. Here's what deans of students told us again and again (Student Affairs Survey, 1997):

"[I'm] dealing with more customer service complaints and possible lawsuits."

"[I have] less of an educational role and more of an administrative, legalistic, paternalistic role."

"[I am] more focused on impact of potential liability now, more concerned with legal versus moral outcomes, especially as relates to student behavior and development."

"I'm spending more time with legal counsel."

"Legal considerations have increased."

"[I] need more legal expertise."

"[There is] more focus on legal and judicial issues."

"[I am] very concerned about legal issues and implications for the university of decision making by officers."

Consumerism is not new on college campuses; it was certainly palpable in the student interviews conducted in the late 1970s.

Since that time, the characteristics of consumerism in higher education have not really changed either. It is a view of higher education as a business, no different from any other commercial enterprise in which a buyer-seller relationship is said to operate, in this case between students and their colleges. Although presumed to be more genteel than a commercial one, this relationship too is rooted in a philosophy of *caveat emptor*. With regard to college, students as buyers are believed to have the same rights as consumers do with any other commercial enterprise.

The anger of college faculty and staff over this philosophy has not dissipated over the past decade and a half. Colleges and universities like to view themselves and their relationship with students very differently. Institutions of higher learning, with their unique and protected social mission of discovering and disseminating truth, see themselves as distinctly different from businesses. They speak of themselves as communities with a shared commitment to learning, rather than as marketplaces of buyers and sellers with fundamentally conflicting purposes. They pride themselves on their long history of social responsibility, nonprofit status, and high ethical standards. Therefore, faculty and administrators tend to perceive the student emphasis on rights as a sense of entitlement.

For all this continuity, consumerism today is radically different from what it was two decades ago. The starkest change is in the forces animating it. In the 1970s, America was living through the post-Watergate era; confidence in all social institutions had declined. Public opinion polls showed that a rising proportion of Americans felt the nation's social institutions, including government, corporations, and colleges as well, were somewhat immoral or dishonest. This encouraged a certain wariness, a consumer orientation, in dealing with the full range of the country's social organizations (Harris and Associates, 1979).

Initially, the changing mood of the nation also propelled consumerism. America was shifting in the 1970s from a progressive era, with a call for citizen responsibility, to a more conservative era, in which social activism waned and self-concern rose. Americans turned inward, focusing increasingly on "me." This gave further impetus to a consumer mentality (Levine, 1980).

Finally, in a series of widely publicized reports and books beginning with the volume *Unsafe at Any Speed* (1965), Ralph Nader gave consumerism a good name. His work in uncovering corporate and government abuse made a consumer outlook appear not only legitimate but wholly essential. Consumerism became not a selfish preoccupation, but almost a patriotic duty.

In short, the consumerism of the 1970s and 1980s was a reflection of broad changes in how Americans thought about our nation and its institutions. It was not directed specifically at higher education. Most, if not all, of the country's social institutions felt the rising consumerism tide.

This is less true in the 1990s. Higher education has received a good deal of criticism in recent years. There have been scandals over athletics, presidential conduct, uses of government funding, price fixing, questionable research results, and violence on campus. Questions have been raised about rapidly rising college costs, faculty workloads, program quality, the commitment to teaching, and campus politics. As a consequence, the current consumer orientation in higher education is targeted at colleges and universities in particular.

Also fueling the movement is the change in student demographics. With more and more students spending less and less time on campus owing to jobs, part-time attendance, and other responsibilities, there is a growing distance between students and their campuses. It is easier for undergraduates to perceive themselves as consumers rather than as members of a community.

Changing Political Climate

If the forces driving consumerism on campus have shifted, so has the political climate on campus. For the past four decades, student participation in campus governance has been accepted as a fact of academic life. At a majority of colleges and universities, undergraduates are members of the student life committee (95 percent), curriculum committee (57 percent), and committees of the board of trustees (53 percent). They also sit on faculty search committees (79 percent) and occasionally even faculty promotion committees (13 percent) (Student Affairs Survey, 1997). More than nine out of ten chief student affairs officers reported the student role in college governance increased during the 1990s (45 percent) or at least remained the same (46 percent) (Student Affairs Survey, 1997).

Yet in governance, consumerism has been a persistent theme. For example, in a curriculum committee meeting at one California state university we visited, a faculty member criticized the administration for taking "our" money (meaning the faculty's) to fund a new program. A student politely but firmly responded, "Please remember it is not your money. It is ours." The faculty member could only smile weakly in return.

The irony—perhaps a reflection of students' decreasing involvement in college life—is that although student power in governance has increased, undergraduates are less interested in being involved in campus governance than in the past. A small minority of undergraduates continue to want voting power or control over admissions decisions, faculty appointments, bachelor's degree requirements, and the content of courses, but a decreasing proportion desire similar roles in residential regulations and undergraduate discipline, areas in which students would seem most likely to want control. Overall, the proportion of students who want voting or controlling roles in institutional governance is at its lowest level in a quarter century (Table 3.1).

Similarly, undergraduates are not voting in student elections. The 1978 Student Affairs Survey found median undergraduate voting rates to be a low 26 to 30 percent in campus elections. In 1997, the proportion had decreased even further to 11 to 15 percent, with a modal voting rate of 6 to 10 percent (Student Affairs Surveys, 1978, 1997).

Table 3.1. Student attitudes regarding governance: 1969, 1976, 1993.

Areas of governance	Percentage of students wanting control or voting power		
	1969	1976	1993
Undergraduate admissions	24	26	25
Faculty appointment and promotion	22	29	29
Bachelor's degree requirements	29	25	24
Provision and content of course	42	32	33
Residence hall regulations	77	70	63
Student discipline	73	64	52
Average	45	41	38

Source: Undergraduate Surveys (1969, 1976, 1993).

By contrast, at the same time undergraduates in rising numbers were saying that they did not want colleges interfering with their lives. In percentages far higher even than in the 1960s, students today are proclaiming that they have a right to engage in campus protest, and that colleges do not have the right to bar speakers from campus. Nor do they believe their fellow students have the right to bar speakers, even those with offensive views (Table 3.2).

At first blush, students' disinterest in campus governance and their strong desire for autonomy seem to be in conflict. In actuality, they are quite consistent. These are the attitudes most of us hold with regard to the commercial enterprises we patronize. We don't want to be bothered with running the bank or the supermarket; we simply want them to do their jobs and do them well—give us consumers what we need without hassles or headaches. That is, help the consumers and don't get in their way. Students today are saying precisely the same things about their colleges.

Hand in hand with this perspective has come a change in campus politics. Traditional student political organizations have declined in importance. There are few right-wing or left-wing groups at colleges (Table 3.3). Student lobbies, particularly statewide student

Table 3.2. Student attitudes regarding campus politics: 1969, 1976, 1993.

	Percentage agreeing		
Political activity	1969	1976	1993
Student demonstrations have no place on a college campus.	29	36	18
College officials have the right to ban persons with extreme views from speaking on campus.	32	24	22
Students have a right to prevent individuals with offensive views from speaking on campus.	—	—	34

Source: Undergraduate Surveys (1969, 1976, 1993).

associations that seek to influence government higher education funding or policy, have declined in number and, even more important, in impact during the 1980s and 1990s. In the seventies, the California State University student lobby was able to boast that no piece of legislation it opposed had ever been enacted. This is no longer true. In the current era of decreasing government confidence in and support for higher education, student lobbies are simply less effective. In 1978, 22 percent of the nation's campuses belonged to a student lobby, and future expansion was widely expected. Today, 18 percent of colleges and universities are members (Table 3.3).

Public interest research groups, called PIRGs, have also faded in prominence. Created by Ralph Nader in 1970 and endorsed by President Carter in 1979, their aim is to engage college students in researching social problems and working constructively to solve them, usually by legislation, lobbying, media attention, public education, and community organizing. During the Carter presidency, one of every nine colleges and universities had a PIRG chapter. Today, the numbers stand at less than one in twelve (Table 3.3).

The reasons for the decline in PIRG membership are more complicated than for student lobbies. One basic reality is that every generation of college students likes to create its own organizations. As

Table 3.3. Political organizations on campus: 1969, 1978, 1992, 1997.

Type of political organization	Percentage of campuses reporting			
	1969	1978	1992	1997
Leftist groups	9	8	6	3
Students for a Democratic Society (SDS)	16	—	—	—
Rightist groups	10	4	7	2
Student lobbies	—	22	18	13
Public interest research groups (PIRGs)	—	11	7	8
Young Democrats	44	30	37	36
College Republicans	43	28	40	40

Note: 1969 percentages obtained from 1978 surveys.
Source: Student Affairs Surveys (1978, 1992, 1997).

far as student-run political or reform organizations go, undergraduates have not accepted past generations' hand-me-downs. The old groups lack vitality. A college generation is seven years long and consists of four classes of students who were on campus when an activity began, plus the three classes of students who subsequently attended college with one or more of the founding classes. PIRGs have survived more than three generations. That's a long time, and an impressive record.

But PIRGs are experiencing competition from newer, more sharply focused student organizations. As umbrella groups, PIRGs may engage in research and reform activities responding to issues involving government, the nonprofit sector, or profit-making corporations. What focus they do have might be on, say, voter rights, tenant rights, consumer rights, animal rights, civil rights, and so on. Given the issue orientation of current college students, the comprehensive approach of PIRGs means they are finding themselves less attractive than in the past. Environmental groups such as SEAC, which use the same research and advocacy techniques that made PIRGs new and different, have become a particularly appealing alternative for undergraduates.

The only traditional political organizations in ascendency on campus in recent years have been the national political parties. Today, College Republicans or Young Democrats are found at about two-fifths of institutions. This is a greater number of chapters than in the 1970s or 1980s and is beginning to approach 1969 levels (Table 3.3). The experience of campus chapters, however, seems to have less to do with student interest than with the interests of the national political parties. In the presidential elections of 1992 and 1996, the Republicans and Democrats both sought to win over the colleges and made a substantial effort to seed the campuses with clubs. But the clubs have not had any notable impact on campus politics. In fact, at none of the campuses visited or surveyed in this study did students or their deans describe the Democratic or Republican groups as influential in college life.

The Rise of Support and Advocacy Groups

Traditional campus political groups have given way to a relatively new breed of organization, which might be called support and advocacy groups. In one form or another, such organizations have been with higher education since at least the nineteenth century, when Christian students banded together to support themselves and their religion and when women enrolling at newly coeducational colleges came together seeking refuge and reform in a hostile environment. Historically, groups like these have served very different purposes, one social and the other political. Socially, they have been places where students who saw themselves as marginal or different could find people like themselves. These groups have promised a comfort zone, where feelings could be shared and time could be spent with people who had similar values and experiences. They have offered emotional support, friendship, and entertainment—in short, an antidote to isolation. At bottom, these organizations have had the potential of becoming "homes," in the best sense of the word.

Politically, they have also served as special interest groups. Given the perceived marginal status of their members, they have often acted as advocates, identifying problems the members faced, educating both members and the larger college community about those problems, and seeking remedies.

Both functions of these support and advocacy groups, social and political, fit the present well. With students spending less time on campus than in the past, the notion of a convenient home or comfort zone is appealing. Similarly, the advocacy role is a natural outgrowth of the student consumer mentality. So it is not surprising that support and advocacy groups are booming on campus today. More than two out of three institutions of higher learning (69 percent) now have such groups. Black, women, and international student associations can be found on a majority of campuses. More than one-third have Latino, gay, and Asian American organizations. And more than one-fifth have multicultural, Native American, disabled student, and men's clubs (Table 3.4).

No type of student organization is growing more quickly than support and advocacy groups. Seven out of every ten campuses (69 percent) reported increases in their membership during the 1990s (Student Affairs Survey, 1997). The modern roots for these groups stretch back to the 1960s and the rise of black student associations. By 1969, nearly one-half of all colleges (46 percent) in the country had an African American organization. In the seventies, the focus shifted to gender. Black groups experienced a slight increase, but the number of campuses with women's organizations nearly doubled, reaching about one-half of all colleges and universities (48 percent) by 1978. In the 1980s and 1990s, groups concerned with race, ethnicity, sexual orientation, and disabilities mushroomed. Native American clubs and Latino groups doubled, and gay and lesbian associations more than tripled (Table 3.4).

The distribution of support and advocacy groups varies sharply from institution to institution. For example, all doctoral-granting institutions in the study reported having black affinity groups, while only 49 percent of four-year colleges and 39 percent of community

Table 3.4. Support and advocacy groups on campus: 1969, 1978, 1992, 1997.

Groups	Percentage of campuses reporting			
	1969	1978	1992	1997
Black	46	58	68	55
Women	27	48	49	51
Latino or Chicano	13	22	41	43
Native American	6	13	21	27
Gay	2	11	35	40
International	—	—	69	68
Disabled	—	—	35	32
Asian American	—	—	34	36
Multicultural	—	—	32	31
Men	—	—	21	14
Racial or ethnic	—	—	—	41

Note: 1969 percentages obtained from 1978 surveys.
Source: Student Affairs Surveys (1978, 1992, 1997).

colleges had them. In general, affinity groups declined as the degree level of institutions declined. The same was true of institutional selectivity. As selectivity decreased, so did the presence of support and advocacy groups (Student Affairs Survey, 1997).

Given the changing political landscape of the campuses, we asked student focus groups, student leaders, and deans of students which were the most powerful groups on campus today. The most common response to the question was a pause, a furrowed brow, and an explanation of why the question was so difficult to answer:

"I've spent the last three years trying to figure that out. I haven't seen too many strong groups."

"Groups come and go. They may be strong one year and nonexistent the next. There is no consistency. There is so much turnover in membership."

"No one mobilizes the whole campus."

"Student leaders seem to have disappeared."

"It is hard to say, because student groups are not that powerful."

"There are not many cohesive groups."

When pushed to name a powerful group, more than nine out of ten of the students we surveyed and interviewed said "student government." This was a huge increase over what we had been told in 1979; the percentage of people citing student government had jumped by more than half (Table 3.5).

Among deans of students, the proportion naming student government was only slightly less: 78 percent of deans of four-year colleges and 52 percent at two-year schools (Student Affairs Survey, 1997). What made this overwhelming answer particularly confusing and unexpected is that campus interest in student government is low and declining, certainly as measured by voting rates. More than this, the majority of student government leaders we interviewed (64 percent) said they had little power to influence their campuses. One student government president put it this way: "I can't wait until my term ends. Student government is a joke; we are not leaders. No one cares what we say or do." The same attitude, though usually stated more moderately, was expressed time and again as a student government president lamented his or her inability to mobilize the student body, to make them care about issues, or even to find a way to communicate with students or get them to listen. Another said, "Sometimes I just want to shake them and scream 'listen to me.'" In many respects, the suggestion that the student government was the most powerful group on campus may be more a reflection of the lack of influence of any other group than it is of the impact of student government.

Complaints of student apathy are not new. They have been perennial since the earliest colleges. The population of colleges and universities is transitory; students graduate each year, and new

Table 3.5. The most powerful student groups on campus, according to students: 1979, 1993.

	Percentage reporting	
Groups	1979	1993
Student government	60	93
African American	37	36
Campus newspaper	33	46
Fraternities and sororities	26	50
Latino students	11	7
Residence halls	11	11
Women	11	4
Hillel	7	—
Athletes	7	—
Radio	7	4
Minority or multicultural	7	14
Volunteers	—	21
Environment	—	14
Gay and lesbian	—	14
International	—	14
Ethnic	—	14

Source: Campus Site Visits (1979, 1993).

students arrive on campus. This means campus groups rise and fall annually with the changes in available leadership and shifting student interests, as was the case with student lobbies and PIRGs.

Interestingly, when deans were asked to name the newest student groups on campus, the most common answers were clubs related to majors, fitness, religion, politics, and the arts. When asked to name clubs that had disappeared in recent years, they named groups focused on religion, social issues, majors, politics, fitness, and Greek life (Student Affairs Survey, 1997). The overlap is striking. More than illustrating a trend, it illustrates the fragility of student organizations.

The growing percentage of students attending college part-time and the declining proportion who live on, and build their lives around, the campus exacerbate the ephemeral character of clubs and groups. Added to this reality is the mitotic nature of current student clubs and groups. At a rather startling rate, student organizations are dividing into smaller and smaller units. For instance, on one campus we visited, the undergraduate business club had split up by gender, race, student geographic origin, and finally sexual orientation, leaving the university with an assortment of business clubs, including organizations for women, African Americans, Koreans, and gays and lesbians, among others! According to deans of students, 8 percent of the nation's colleges and universities had ten or more each of African American and international student organizations on campus, 5 percent had ten or more Asian American groups, and 3 percent had ten or more women's groups. In fact, thirty-five campuses had more than twenty international student groups, and thirty-one had more than twenty women's organizations (Student Affairs Survey, 1997). We talk about some of the reasons for this mitosis, a variation on the local orientation of students, in Chapter Four.

The mitotic effect is that not only are student groups proliferating, but the membership of each is necessarily declining. The expanding numbers of organizations mean that there are more and more groups with tiny constituencies vying for political influence on campus. Their shrinking size makes it increasingly difficult for them to find effective leaders annually and to maintain much in the way of continuity in leadership.

The Resurgence of Student Activism

So it would be reasonable to expect campus activism to be on the decline. But this is not what is happening. Student protest is booming. In 1969, near the height of campus unrest, 28 percent of undergraduates reported participating in a demonstration. By 1976, the proportion had dropped to 19 percent. Today, it stands at 25 percent, nearly a return to the sixties' level of activism (Undergraduate Surveys, 1969, 1976, 1993).

The profile of students who participate in demonstrations has not changed very much over time. Those who are full-time, traditional-age, residential, at selective universities, minority, and whose parents attended college are most likely to protest. What is worth noting, however, is that there is no gap between men and women, even though men were historically more prone to protest. But there is a huge gap between races. Today, African American students have on average half again the rate of involvement in protest activities of any other demographic group on campus (Table 3.6).

The nature of student activism has changed significantly. In the 1960s and early 1970s, campus protests emphasized two common issues: Vietnam and civil rights. As a result, the sixties' protests were very visible and national in scope. In contrast, current student activism focuses largely on local issues and has done so since the late 1970s. This has the effect of making protest activities, in the main, campus specific and, as a consequence, almost invisible (Table 3.7).

A whopping 93 percent of site visit campuses had experienced student unrest in the past two years. There were two principal issues, both of which were consumer concerns as we define the term: multiculturalism (on 48 percent of the campuses) and the rising costs of college (37 percent). Multiculturalism far overshadowed any other issue, particularly when such related concerns as gender equity, sexual orientation, free speech, and civil rights were added to the mix (Table 3.8). In general, the impetus for protests was campus based, not externally fueled. That explains, to a large extent, the discrepancy between high student interest in preserving the environment and the low level of student unrest centered on this issue. The dean of students at Southern Methodist University in Texas captured the thinking of most of the student affairs officers interviewed in saying, "Students seem active only on local issues that affect them and their lives on campus."

There was only one notable exception, which was mentioned earlier in this study: the initial Rodney King trial verdict and the

Table 3.6. Characteristics of student demonstrators: 1993.

Characteristics	Percentage reporting
Type of college attended	
Two-year college	22
Four-year college	26
University	29
Attendance	
Attend full-time	26
Attend part-time	22
Gender	
Male	25
Female	25
Residential status	
Resident	29
Commuter	23
Race	
Caucasian	23
Black	41
Hispanic	26
Asian American	23
Total minorities	33
Age	
Under 25	26
Over 25	23
Parents' education	
Attended college	27
Didn't attend college	21

Source: Undergraduate Survey (1993).

rioting in Los Angeles that followed. More than two out of five of the site visit campuses had experienced some form of activism as a consequence. As a rule, it was peaceful (marches, vigils, town meetings, forums, and rallies), but there was at least one instance of property damage. In general, the activism was short in duration, but at two institutions, Wellesley and Carleton, it turned into a longer-term examination of race on campus.

The experience of the site visit schools revealed that several issues emerging as causes for activism were either absent in the past

Table 3.7. The causes of student unrest: 1969, 1978, 1992, 1997.

	Percentage of campuses reporting			
Causes	1969	1978	1992	1997
Vietnam	68	—	—	—
Minority issues (race, gender, sexual orientation, physical disability)	35	12	24	39
Campus rules of student behavior	22	11	4	2
Faculty and staff employment	12	18	8	11
ROTC or draft	10	—	—	—
Administrative policies and procedures	4	17	7	17
Institutional facilities	3	19	—	2
Institutional services	3	12	2	5
Student finances (fees, financial aid, and budget cuts)	2	20	27	29
Sexual harassment	—	—	5	5
Environment	—	—	1	1

Note: 1969 percentages obtained from 1978 surveys.
Source: Student Affairs Surveys (1978, 1992, 1997).

or have grown substantially in importance in recent years. The most dramatic change was in issues related to gender. At St. John's University in New York and Concordia College in Oregon, the focus was on rape and sexual assault. Students at Roosevelt University and Oglethorpe were concerned with sexual harassment. Choice and birth control were issues at Catholic University and Drake. The negative portrayal of women by a fraternity was the touch point at Wayne State. In total, 37 percent of the site visit schools experienced protests over gender issues.

Another set of issues that are booming on college campuses relates to gay and lesbian rights. For instance, at the University of Minnesota, gay and lesbian students crashed a board of trustees meeting and handcuffed themselves to trustee chairs to protest institutionalized policies on homosexuality. At Portland Community

Table 3.8. Specific causes of campus protests: 1993.

Causes of protest	Percentage of campuses reporting
Multiculturalism	48
The first Rodney King verdict	41
Tuition and fees	37
Gender issues	37
Gay and lesbian issues	15
Free speech	15
The Gulf War	7
Student regulations	7
Academic changes	7
Firing of faculty or staff	7
Access to college	7
Fraternity and sorority policy	4
Animal rights	4
Campus speakers	4

Source: Campus Site Visits (1993).

College, a ballot measure mobilized students to support gay rights. The appointment of a lesbian dorm counselor at Wellesley was a cause of activism there. At Oglethorpe, use of the word "faggot" resulted in demonstrations. Fifteen percent of the site visit campuses had experienced recent protests over issues of sexual orientation.

Free speech was also a hot area. At Drake University, students protested an appearance by conservative activist Phyllis Schlafly. The issue at the University of Texas at Arlington was a Johnny Reb mascot; a confederate flag sparked protest at Morris Brown College. Emerson College had a demonstration when a student wore blackface to a costume party. At Concordia College and Catholic University, there was an uproar over condoms being attached to campus newspapers.

Changes in protest tactics have been at least as dramatic as the shifts in the issues, as shown in Table 3.9.

Table 3.9. Tactics of student protest: 1969, 1978, 1992, 1997.

Tactics	Percentage of campuses reporting			
	1969	1978	1992	1997
Demonstration	39	13	33	34
Petition of redress	24	20	33	37
Threat of violence	20	3	15	22
Taking over building	15	—	6	3
Strike	14	1	2	—
Intentional destruction of property	12	1	4	5
Taking issues to court	4	6	10	15
Other (lobbying, demanding hearings, educational activities)	4	27	12	10
Going public	—	—	27	46
Refusal to pay tuition	—	—	<1	5
Disrupting class	—	—	12	17
E-mail	—	—	—	16

Note: 1969 percentages obtained from 1978 surveys.
Source: Student Affairs Surveys (1978, 1992, 1997).

In contrast to the 1960s, use of more disruptive forms of protest is down: building takeovers, destruction of property, and strikes (though each has increased slightly since the 1970s). Classroom disruption is a very real exception now, although it was not mentioned in previous surveys. Demonstrations have risen 150 percent since the 1970s and are now almost at the same level as in the 1960s. Petitions, litigation, and threats of violence have surpassed occurrences in the 1960s, but the true growth area is going public with an issue, that is, seeking press and external exposure. This is the unique form of protest of the 1990s and by far the most popular; it did not show up to any significant degree in the earlier surveys. In fact, the combination of petitions, litigation, demonstrations, and going public is a direct translation of the most popular consumer tactics to student activism. Lastly, the e-mail protest, which barrages an office with critical missives, is another invention of the 1990s.

Deans of students said, regardless of the tactics used, students were more polite than in the past but still insistent. At the University of Colorado, the vice president for student affairs told of undergraduates calling to let her know the time of a demonstration and asking for advice to ensure they were in compliance with campus rules. This was not unusual; similar stories were told on many campuses. As the dean of students at the University of California, Santa Barbara (UCSB), told us, the watchword of today's students is "no surprises."

A demonstration on the UCSB campus is a good example. Students were protesting a series of Latino issues, ranging from the failure to hire a Chicano faculty member to rising tuition costs and decreasing access for Hispanic students. A campus coalition group called El Congreso Latino brought together twenty or so distinct organizations, including women's groups and the pre-law association, to sponsor a demonstration. The demonstration itself was designed to appeal to both students and the local community. It included an affirmation of Latino culture through poetry readings, art exhibits, seminars, and a reception. In addition, students took over a building from 9:00 A.M. to 5:00 P.M., coordinating their activities with campus security and student affairs. There was also a press conference. The protesters controlled events by means of walkie talkies and armband identification, policed their own demonstration, and had paramedics lined up to take care of any medical problems that might occur. Between eighteen hundred and two thousand students showed up. As a student affairs staffer at UCSB said, "They pushed right up to the limit, but didn't cross the line."

The protesters made sure that the university knew there were a lot of students who cared about their issue. They told the university they were willing to push the issue publicly if UCSB was unwilling to resolve it privately. They made sure the students who participated had a good time and would come back again. The protest at UCSB epitomized campus activism in the 1990s. The issue was local; the tactics were pure consumerism.

Today's student consumerism, then, as it defines campus politics, is more than just a state of mind. It is a philosophy of governance, concerned with student rights versus college and university rights. It is based on a buyer-seller relationship in a collegiate marketplace governed by a philosophy of *caveat emptor*. It is active as well as reactive, seeking rights of choice, safety, and information in addition to redress for perceived wrongs.

Today's students are less interested in participating in traditional campus governance, however, and there are few powerful student groups on campus. Instead, colleges are witnessing the multiplication of support and advocacy groups, designed to advance the causes and needs of individuals and collegiate subgroups more than the student body as a whole. Activism is on the rise once again, but the tactics employed have changed from the forceful, confrontational approaches of the sixties to the more contemporary (and legal) tactics of the consumer movement. The two most common causes for protest today are multiculturalism and the price of college. The next chapter deals with the first of these issues.

4

$\cdot\ \cdot$

Multiculturalism
The Campus Divided

"People say to me that I'm overreacting—that there's been so much progress since the 1960s—but I've seen people almost walk off the sidewalk to avoid walking too close to me."

Black student

"I'm conscious of the fact that I don't stand to gain from multiculturalism."

White student

The 1990s produced an avalanche of front-page news articles, magazine cover stories, instant bestsellers, pop movies, and network exposés on multiculturalism, diversity, and political correctness. So it's a little surprising that more than three out of five students on campus today (Undergraduate Survey, 1993) say that

- They have at least one friend of another race (69 percent)
- They feel comfortable expressing unpopular or controversial opinions on campus (65 percent)
- They are comfortable with interracial dating (64 percent)
- They feel a sense of community on campus (62 percent)
- They do not feel more comfortable socializing with students of their own race (60 percent)

The logical conclusion is that the media got the story wrong, except deans of students say they didn't. A majority of deans at four-year colleges (Student Affairs Survey, 1997) say that:

- The climate on campus can be described as politically correct (60 percent)

- Civility has declined on the college campus (57 percent)

- Students of different racial and ethnic groups do not often socialize together (56 percent)

- Reports of sexual harassment have increased (55 percent)

- Students feel uncomfortable expressing unpopular or controversial opinions (54 percent)

More than two-fifths (41 percent) of the deans say that there is more tension on campus regarding issues of diversity, and 34 percent report a greater sense of victimization among students on campus today. In fact, diversity issues are the main cause of conflict between students on three out of five campuses (62 percent) (Student Affairs Survey, 1997).

A Painful Subject

So what is going on? Multiculturalism is a painful subject on campus today. Students don't want to discuss it. In group interviews, students were more willing to tell us intimate details of their sex lives than to discuss race relations on campus. In fact, when focus groups were asked about the state of race relations at their college, the usual response was silence. In one instance, no one spoke for more than two minutes until the interviewer, unnerved by the quiet, broke the silence. The dirty words on college campuses no longer have four letters. They are six-letter words like "racist," "sexist," and "homophobic," which is even longer. In this superheated environment, students are reluctant to discuss the topics of multiculturalism in general and race in particular with strangers. When prodded about race relations in diversified focus groups, students usually attempted to say things were OK, although tension levels in the room would rise perceptively when the question was asked and reasked. Body language and facial expressions changed, smiles disappeared. If students of color in the focus group were willing to accept the conclusion that everything was fine, the topic was glossed over. If not, a tortuous, often angry, conversation, with lots of silences followed. There was a tendency for students to look down at the table at which they were seated rather than at each other.

In private, individual conversations were very different. Few students were quiet. Some said campus race relations were "good," "better," "OK," or "fine," but many more used words like "scary," "frightening," "sad," "angry," "embattled," "isolated," "divided," "frustrating," "heated," "explosive," "confused," "a mess," and "hopeless" to describe them. They were more concerned and negative at four-year colleges than at two-year schools, and at residential institutions than at nonresidential institutions. This means that students were most troubled about race relations on those campuses in which diverse groups had the greatest opportunity for sustained contact.

Individual conversations with students of color and whites were very different. Students of color regularly said they felt uncomfortable on campus: "I feel like an unwelcome guest at a party rather than a member of the family." This was especially true for African American students.

Students of color complained about being continually asked to educate whites about minority issues. One junior said, "In my classes, I'm always being asked how African Americans view this or that." She went on to say that she was not the universal African American but rather just one person being forced into a very small box. Others said that they did not come to college to educate whites, that it was not their job. They are paying a lot of money and giving up a lot of time for their own education.

Students of color resented the stereotypes they regularly encountered. A student laughed somewhat bitterly and said that she had been asked several times what it was like to grow up in a ghetto. She had grown up in Scarsdale, one of the most affluent suburbs in the United States. (She added that she guessed it was a ghetto of sorts, but not the type her classmates imagined.) An international student at a black college talked of a similar experience at her institution, where fellow undergraduates wondered what it was like to live in a hut. She said her family had a larger, more modern home than did most of her classmates.

Across the United States, another student told of classmates asking if they could touch her hair. They had never seen African American hair up close before. A Vietnamese undergraduate said other students never invited her to the movies or to go shopping. They only socialized with her when they needed help with their calculus homework. A woman from the South Bronx could not believe her classmates were asking questions like, "How do you keep your comb in your hair?" "Do people really get shot on the streets?" and "Do cops really break into apartments?" The most common complaint among students of color was that whites always mixed them up. They called them by each other's names even when they did not look anything alike, giving the impression that whites classified students of color principally in terms of their race.

Among whites, attitudes about race and multiculturalism varied by 180 degrees. A student newspaper reporter at the University of Colorado brilliantly described the poles that emerged in our conversations with white students: "On the part of whites, there is either a sense of rejection—'we had a civil rights movement; why do they keep bringing it up?'—or a tremendous sense of guilt. They want to be like Kevin Costner in *Dances with Wolves*."

Across this spectrum from rejection to engagement, students expressed a wealth of emotions, but the most common feelings were confusion and uncertainty. Regardless of how students diagnosed multicultural realities on campus, few knew what to do about them:

"We have an African American staff member on the news-paper. He is doing a story on Native Americans. In the office, he talks all the time about his dislike for Jews and Hispanics. Yet he's been removed from being called a racist because he's black. Does this make any sense?"

"Is race a legitimate concern?"

"Sometimes I think black men are just mad at me for not see-ing all their issues and problems."

"I don't know how to approach [race]. I am afraid some blacks don't like whites. I feel like I'd love to apologize for the injus-tices of the past. It's not right."

"Most problems here are because everyone has a mirror to their face and sees the world only in terms of their issues. There is a seventeen-year-old black student on the paper. She is from a wealthy family. She takes up the torch of every black issue and sees everything in terms of race. She thinks all Europeans are the same. We are not. My ancestors (from Poland) never enslaved black Americans. . . . I don't know what we do about [this]."

"The tension I see on campus about race is because of myths and misconceptions about people. . . . Southeastern Michigan is obsessed with race. White is always right. Nobody knows what's good for you but you. I hate that."

"I really don't understand it."

Tension regarding diversity and difference runs high all across college life. Overt incidents—name calling, graffiti writing, and physical abuse—are actually quite rare, though most campuses seem to experience them at least periodically. During the 1990s, 24 per-cent of colleges and universities surveyed had seen rises in racial hate incidents, and 31 percent had increases in gender incidents. The increase was greater at four-year colleges than at two-year col-leges (Table 4.1).

Table 4.1. Institutions reporting change in the number of hate incidents on campus, by two-year and four-year institutions: 1997.

| | Percentage of campuses reporting change | | | | | | | | |
| | Increased | | | Remained the same | | | Decreased | | |
Type of incident	2-year	4-year	Total	2-year	4-year	Total	2-year	4-year	Total
Racial hate	11	32	24	63	41	58	18	17	18
Gender hate	23	40	31	53	47	49	23	16	19

Source: Student Affairs Survey (1997).

However, the targets of such behavior are diffuse—remarkably diffuse. In fact, no difference seemed immune from such attacks—race, gender, religion, sexual orientation, nationality, disability, you name it. But the most vicious graffiti and name calling is usually reserved for women and gays. Observed one student: "If PC condemns gay bashing, then people are hypocritical. You can get away with gay bashing. Even liberal friends say, 'I wouldn't want a gay person teaching my children.'"

A new twist in such incidents comes in the form of hate messages on the Internet or through in-house computer systems. Recent reports find e-mail is being used increasingly as a forum for the hard-to-prosecute activity of "flame mail," intended to harass or threaten fellow students. At the University of California at Irvine, for example, a former student has been accused of threatening fifty-eight students, ten of whom have filed criminal charges ("E-Mail . . . ," 1997).

Hate incidents can and do cause explosions on campus, but they are not the stuff that fuels the daily tensions. Far more powerful is the everyday grind of collegiate life. The sources of friction over diversity and difference are omnipresent, found in the very classrooms in which students study. Again and again, undergraduates described their classes in a manner reminiscent of our focus group conversations. For example, an African American student at Wayne State said it was impossible to talk about diversity in her courses: "In class you don't make remarks in terms of ethnicity—no, no, you can't say anything about the topic." A white student at Southern Methodist University offered exactly the same conclusion for the opposite reason: "African Americans are so adamant about their opinions, whites don't speak in class." At Wellesley, students criticized black professors for anti-Semitism. At the University of the District of Columbia, black students criticized Jews for racism. At the University of Colorado, a Hispanic undergraduate said the only place where he felt comfortable was in his ethnic studies course—while a white student complained that no matter how hard she tried, she was not allowed to fit into the same ethnic studies course.

Comparable frictions exist in residence halls. At Drake, asking a student to turn down his music became an argument over race. A dorm meeting at Catholic University on improving campus security turned into an attack on the local black community. In residence, students live very closely, and race is a recurrent, daily, personal rub.

Tensions are fed by the posters students see on campus walls too. At the University of California, Santa Barbara, women students complained of fraternity banners showing fashionably dressed men and scantily clad women, with the title, "More Bounce to the Ounce." A student election poster at Oglethorpe University had an African American caricature and a black English caption. Destruction and defacing of unpopular posters was a complaint at most campuses. Some of this activity was especially ugly. Across a women's bulletin board filled with announcements of events and routine messages between students, someone had written in big, black letters, "Women are a piece of shit." At Manhattan College, a series of beautiful cloth banners, created by students for women's week, were slashed, cut, and painted over.

Campus events often had a chilling effect too. Talent shows brought out students in blackface from coast to coast, from Emerson College in Boston to UC, Santa Barbara. A white student at the Illinois Institute of Technology dressed up as Aunt Jemima for Halloween, and fraternity members at Georgia Tech wore Confederate uniforms for Old South Day. Campus speakers also brought home the issue of race. A student at St. John's talked of a rap singer who said, "Kill the white man." He was shocked when his schoolmates applauded. Students of color at several colleges expressed outrage at neoconservative speakers who were critical of minorities.

Hiring practices increased tensions as well. At Portland Community College, hiring a Vietnamese man over a white man resulted in a lawsuit and a campus brouhaha. At the University of California, Santa Barbara, the opposite occurred: rejection of a Hispanic faculty candidate for a white caused a campus demonstration.

The sorts of tests colleges require raised the issue of diversity as well. At Wayne State University, when a black student failed the English proficiency test she had taken several times, resultant cries of cultural bias arose, despite historically high passage rates by students of color.

Day-to-day activities also highlighted the differences on campus. At Catholic University, campus security was charged with disproportionately stopping black students to ask for identification. A student government officer there created a scene as well when he challenged the parents of a black student visiting the library because he thought they looked out of place.

Causes of Multicultural Tension

Four characteristics of current students exacerbate these conditions.

Preoccupation with Differences

The first is that today's undergraduates think of themselves in terms of their differences rather than their commonalities. When students were interviewed for the prior study in the late 1970s, they were asked to describe themselves. In the main, they emphasized common generational characteristics or values: being career oriented, wanting material success, caring about appearance and self, being politically disinterested, and so on. But conversations with current students were remarkably different. When faced with the same question as their predecessors, they emphasized the characteristics that made them unique or different: race, gender, geography, sexual orientation, ethnicity, and religion. For example, one student said he grew up in a small town in which he was one of a handful of Asian Americans in his school. He said he never thought of his Asian roots as being important until he got to college. By the end of his freshman year, he realized it was the most important aspect of his being. That was until his junior year, when he decided being Korean

American was even more important. When asked to describe him-self, he told the interviewer he was a Korean American; to ascer-tain other characteristics and interests required additional questions. In this environment, students both perceive and value their differ-ences more than their commonalities.

The fact of the matter is that the "real" differences among stu-dents are huge. There are great divides by gender. There are even bigger and more dramatic differences by race.

As one might expect, there is a gap between men and women on gender issues. Women see higher levels of discrimination, vul-nerability, and need for redress than men do (Table 4.2).

The same gap exists in race issues by members of different racial groups, as shown in Table 4.3. But here the gap is even larger. Although there is a split between minorities and majorities, the real differences are between racial groups. There is, for example, a chasm between blacks and whites, the two groups that were farthest apart

Table 4.2. Gender issues, by gender: 1993.

Gender issues	Percentage agreeing	
	Men	Women
To get ahead in this world, a woman has to be twice as good at what she does as a man.	33	70
Feminism has created more problems than it has solved for American women.	46	31
Sexual discrimination will seriously affect my chances to get a job.	8	36
I worry about becoming a victim of violent crime.	36	54
Women should be given preference for jobs if they have the same qualifications as male applicants.	23	38
Women are apt to charge sexual harassment without legitimate provocation.	38	23

Source: Undergraduate Survey (1993).

Table 4.3. Racial issues, by race: 1993.

Racial issues	Percentage agreeing					
	White	Black	Hispanic	Asian American	Total minorities
Racial discrimination will seriously affect my chances to get a job.	8	67	28	53	53
Most American colleges and universities are racist whether they mean to be or not.	31	57	37	45	49
Ethnic studies programs should be administered and controlled by people of that ethnic group.	48	70	61	57	64
More minority group undergraduates should be admitted, even if it means utilizing different admission standards.	25	55	48	43	50
I am more comfortable socializing with members of my own race.	38	53	26	46	44
We hear too much about the rights of minorities and not enough about the rights of majorities.	60	13	40	34	25
This country has not made real progress toward racial equality in the last five years.	47	75	55	58	66
Racial integration of public elementary schools should be achieved, even if it requires busing.	46	65	59	63	63

Source: Undergraduate Survey (1993).

in the study. On average, there was a 30-percentage-point difference between their responses to questions dealing with race. In contrast, the spread between Asian Americans and whites was 19
percentage points and between Hispanics and whites 14 percentage
points. This means that Hispanics were slightly closer in opinion to
whites than to blacks.

These differences over gender and race are only the beginning.
Sex and color also divide students on political and social policy
issues (Table 4.4).

Indeed, there is nothing new in the existence of a gender gap.
Women are socially and politically more liberal than men. The data
from this study show they are more caring; they are more critical of
social differences, more supportive of civil rights, and less likely to
classify themselves as conservative politically. One of the most
telling consequences of these differences may be the gender split
over Clarence Thomas's Supreme Court confirmation hearings. Less
than one-third of undergraduate males (31 percent) found Anita
Hill, who accused Thomas of sexual harassment, more credible than
Thomas. In contrast, a clear majority of women undergraduates did
(55 percent). However, there was little difference by race.

In terms of race, the division between blacks and whites remains
equally vivid on political and social policy. Blacks possess the same
liberal orientation as women, with one major difference: they are
also more activist. Forty-one percent of black students report having participated in a demonstration, in contrast with 23 percent of
whites.

The political differences between blacks and whites come through
even more strongly when each was presented with a list of twenty-six
well-known personalities. They were asked which people on the list
they rated positively and which they rated negatively. In comparing
the top five negatives and top five positives (Table 4.5), one should
note that all of the names on the black positive list were black.

Three of the five names on the white negative list were black.
Each list had only one name in common: both blacks and whites

Table 4.4. Social issues, by gender and race: 1993.

	Percentage agreeing						
Social issues	Male	Female	White	Black	Hispanic	Asian American	Total minorities
I found Anita Hill's testimony more credible than that of Clarence Thomas.	31	55	44	43	42	51	45
Homosexual males and females should be allowed legally to join the military.	49	68	57	65	67	64	65
The United States was right to send troops to Kuwait in Operation Desert Storm.	76	69	76	49	68	72	59
Economic well-being in this country is unjustly and unfairly distributed.	59	71	63	82	68	66	75
I would describe myself as politically conservative.	33	21	31	9	25	20	15
I would describe myself as politically liberal.	34	43	36	54	38	40	46
I have taken part in a campus demonstration.	25	25	23	41	26	23	33

Source: Undergraduate Survey (1993).

Table 4.5. Personalities perceived as most positive and
most negative, by race: 1993.

Positive perception	
By blacks	By whites
Nelson Mandela	Margaret Thatcher
Malcolm X	Ross Perot
Spike Lee	Magic Johnson
Jesse Jackson	Boris Yeltsin
Magic Johnson	Lee Iacocca
Negative perception	
By blacks	By whites
Ronald Reagan	Ted Kennedy
George Bush	Jesse Jackson
Ross Perot	Malcolm X
Pat Buchanan	Spike Lee
Boris Yeltsin	Pat Buchanan

Source: Undergraduate Survey (1993).

rated Magic Johnson positively, and both ranked Pat Buchanan negatively. However, there was substantial overlap between the negative and positive lists. The white negative list included three names
on the black positive list: Jesse Jackson, Malcolm X, and Spike Lee.
And the black negative list had two names from the white positive
list: Ross Perot and Boris Yeltsin.

In short, the differences between blacks and whites in this exercise greatly overshadowed the commonalities. The heroes of one
were more likely to be the villains of the other, rather than the
names being shared.

It is almost as if people from different groups inhabited different worlds. When asked what was the key or number one social or
political event that influenced their lives, students gave remarkably different answers. The most common responses from men were

the *Challenger* explosion and the Gulf War. In contrast, women answered the *Roe v. Wade* Supreme Court decision on abortion rights (Undergraduate Survey, 1993).

The same phenomenon existed with regard to race. Whites chose *Roe v. Wade*, the *Challenger*, and the Gulf War as key events. Blacks pointed to the Rodney King verdict, the Martin Luther King Jr. assassination, and the release of Nelson Mandela. Hispanics named Rodney King and *Roe v. Wade*. Asian Americans selected the Vietnam War, the Tiananmen Square demonstrations, and Rodney King.

In sum, the racial events that influenced each group were almost entirely and predictably different. Only Rodney King—a racial attack—permeated the entire minority community. It is as if each group grew up and continues to live in a separate world. This may explain why the differences among students loom so much greater than the commonalities.

Mitosis of Student Groups

The second characteristic exacerbating conditions on campus is one suggested by the Korean American student and discussed earlier. It is that the differences among students are getting larger and more focused. The student defined himself initially without reference to ethnicity, then more narrowly in terms of his Asian origins, and finally even more narrowly in regard to his Korean roots. This reflects the process of mitosis of campus clubs and groups discussed in the last chapter. But perhaps more important, the effect is continuously to reduce the proportion of students whom undergraduates define as being "like me" while increasing the group perceived as being "different from me." More and more undergraduates see themselves living in a very lonely world, with few people like them.

Segregation on Campus

The third characteristic is that students systematically misjudge the degree of interaction they have with students who are different from them. Much of American higher education is voluntarily segregated today; even by the most generous of standards, less than a handful of the campuses visited in this study could be described in any other way. More than one-third of all colleges and universities (35 percent) reported that there are locations on campus that belong to particular groups by virtue of squatters' rights. This is true of 29 percent of two-year colleges and 41 percent of four-year colleges (Student Affairs Survey, 1997). Walk into the cafeteria in most colleges and universities, and the tables are separated by race and ethnicity. The larger the campus, the sharper the divisions. At small colleges, there is likely to be a Hispanic or Latino table. At bigger schools, this becomes Puerto Rican, Dominican, Chicano, Colombian, Panamanian, and Jamaican tables. Students across the country described the divisions this way:

"In the cafeteria, sides are literally assigned—one side white, one black, one Asian."—Illinois Institute of Technology

"You look in the dining center. People eat at segregated tables."—University of Northern Iowa

"There is separation at the dining room. Different places on campus are claimed by different groups. The (lower) lounge is black. The other lounge is Hispanic. The engineering lounge is Asian."—Catholic University

"In the dining room, if you see one person, you know the rest at the table."—University of the District of Columbia

"Blacks sit and eat together in the student center. . . . A few incidents have occurred. In the fall, for example, a white freshman sat in the wrong area. . . . It's a serious situation but not volatile. It's not going to erupt imminently."—Georgia Institute of Technology

"I think the races are pretty much separate and happy about it."—Southern Methodist University

"The white students sit in their place. The Arabic-Indian students sit in their place. The black students sit in their place."
—Wayne State University

"[In] dining commons, each group sits alone."—University of California, Santa Barbara

"Groups are isolated on campus. Ethnic kids hang out with their same ethnic groups."—Boston University

Residence halls are a somewhat unusual area of segregation. Not only do they exhibit the voluntary patterns of division characteristic of other parts of the campus, but they also have planned separations. Twenty-seven percent of colleges and universities surveyed have special-interest housing for students, that is, dormitory space earmarked for particular groups. Other residences are reserved on the basis of race, ethnicity, or religion: international students (10 percent), African American students (4 percent), multicultural (2 percent), Latinos (2 percent), Native Americans (1 percent), and by religion (1 percent). But even more of the space is reserved for other purposes, including honors students (8 percent) and specific majors (5 percent), lifestyles and issues (4 percent each), fitness (4 percent), arts (3 percent), sports (2 percent), and leadership (2 percent) (Student Affairs Survey, 1997).

There were two fascinating exceptions to this pattern of dining room segregation. For the most part, except at the very smallest campuses, integrated groups tended to be either athletes or theater people. In both instances, the close working relationships among students in these fields appeared to overcome the perception of difference looming larger than commonality. In reality, even if a quarterback is black and his receiver is white, each needs to be able to count on the other. If Lady Macbeth is an Arab and Macbeth is a Jew, they must still work together if a play is to be performed. Close contact and common goals appeared to be the best stereotype-busters and inducement for integration on campus.

The rules were somewhat different for dating. Thirty-six percent of undergraduates said they were not comfortable with interracial dating and marriage. Whites (39 percent) were less comfortable than blacks (29 percent), Asian Americans (23 percent), and Hispanics (16 percent) (Undergraduate Survey, 1993). This represents a ludicrous situation, in which majorities and minorities do not sit together in public places, but almost two-thirds of all students think it is all right to marry one another. The explanation is that theory and practice diverge: in reality, only 7 percent of the class of '93 reported in 1991 dating a member of another ethnic group during the previous year. Only 27 percent dined with a member of another ethnic group (Higher Education Research Institute, 1992).

In focus groups, the reasons for the disparity became even clearer. When asked whether interracial couples walking across campus holding hands would draw attention or be frowned on, the answer was most likely to be "no" on politically liberal and highly selective campuses and in major metropolitan areas, particularly in the Northeast and West. There are a pair of important caveats here. First, the answers were far from uniform. Students said "yes" and "no" on all kinds of campuses. Second, students reported being most accepting of interracial dating on those campuses on which such behavior was most politically correct. For instance, at Southern Methodist University, where students agreed that interracial dating would be frowned on, there was consensus in the focus group that there are "few instances of it at SMU." One woman student said, "I know if I did [date a nonwhite], my friends would feel very uncomfortable. . . . I would not do it. I guess it's pretty unaccepted." Much of the rest of the focus group nodded in agreement. In contrast, at Boston University, which attracts a more liberal student body, undergraduates thought there would be little reaction to an interracial couple. However, the student newspaper editor said he wrote a supporting article on interracial dating and discussed his experience of dating a black woman. He said he "was verbally attacked" for his views. He concluded that "racism is hidden" at BU.

By way of contrast, there was only one campus in the study on which students thought a same-sex couple would not draw attention or be frowned on. Being antigay was decidedly less hidden than racism.

A number of students talked about their experiences with interracial dating. For many, perhaps most, it was "no big deal," but in general, white women who dated a black man said they had a very hard time. One woman expressed the fears and emotions of her peers, saying, "Everyone on this campus thinks I'm a slut" simply because she would date an African American man.

Frequently, the disapprobation regarding interracial dating was internal. That is, it came from one's own peer group, not the outgroup one was dating into. For example, African American students had a clear set of rules about what dating was permissible and what was not, with little variation from campus to campus. African American students said black women were permitted to date nonblack men, but black men were discouraged from dating non-African American women. The rationale was that black women outnumbered African American men on most campuses. The men were therefore needed by the women as companions, but, because there were so few men, women were allowed to go outside their group for dates.

Dating rules for Asian Americans and Latinos were far less constant. They varied from institution to institution and from coast to coast. However, students spoke knowledgeably and consistently about what rules operated on their own campuses.

Perhaps because of the rules governing socializing and segregation of the campus, students regularly underestimated the degree of interaction they had with people who were different from them. For instance, one of the authors took attendance at school events at several campuses. When Asian American students who had brought a speaker to campus were asked how many whites attended the event, they said whites never attended their activities. When pressured regarding numbers, they indicated that only a handful of whites had been present. However, a count of the audience indicated that at least a third of those attending were Caucasian. After a dance, white students were asked how many blacks had attended. They indicated that blacks did not go to white parties. When pushed, the whites said maybe twenty blacks were present. In reality, the number was closer to fifty.

The most dramatic example of this behavior occurred at Oberlin College. When asked about interracial friendships and dating, students spoke about segregation and said mixing was unusual, this at a campus that prides itself historically on being the first interracial college, and currently on "gender bending" (busting the rules on stereotypical gender behavior). Throughout the entire conversation, a number of interracial couples and groups walked by. In fact, the degree of racial integration was higher on this campus than at most schools, but the students simply did not see it.

This is a troubling situation. It suggests two possibilities. Either students are so convinced of campus segregation that they do not perceive integration even when it occurs or, even worse, when diverse students are in close proximity, they are so isolated that they still do not interact.

A Growing Sense of Victimization

The fourth student characteristic that heightens tensions over diversity is a growing sense of victimization, yet another spur for consumerism. In the 1980s and early 1990s, a majority of four-year-college deans (54 percent) reported that a rising proportion of undergraduates felt they were being disadvantaged to the perceived advantage of other students. When asked in 1997 about the level of victimization during the 1990s, another 41 percent of campus deans reported increases (Student Affairs Surveys, 1992, 1997). Affluent students complained that they were being made to pay higher tuition to support less affluent undergraduates. Poorer students said admissions standards were less rigorous for students who can pay full tuition. Men pointed fingers at women, who, they felt, had preference in entering traditionally male professions, and women pointed back at men, talking of the glass ceiling they experienced. Racial majorities charged that minorities were being advantaged at their expense, and minorities made the reverse claim. International students were critical of domestic populations and vice versa. One religious group complained about the preferential treatment given the next.

The bottom line is that the American college is increasingly a place in which students feel they are being treated unfairly and others are profiting at their expense. This perception, in combination with a preoccupation with differences, adds up to an environment in which the zone of indifference is disappearing. Conversations or actions that might normally be ignored or have no underlying meaning or import take on great significance in a world in which students feel they are being victimized because of their differences. Tolerance is becoming a scarce commodity. Students have hair triggers where issues of difference are concerned, whether they are real or merely imagined.

Add to this the fact that we live in a time in which the focus is on people's differences, not their commonalities; perceived and real isolation between diverse groups seems unbridgeable; and a mitosis within groups appears to be accelerating. In this environment, the very real danger is that our campuses will become Hobbesian worlds of each against all.

At more than one-third of the campuses visited, campuswide groups—committees, commissions, and task forces—had been created to respond to these realities. In increasing numbers and largely by accretion, colleges and universities are infusing diversity into the curriculum (Levine and Cureton, 1992). But few, if any, seemed to be making a dent in the topic. Multiculturalism remains the most unresolved issue on campus today.

. . . .

5

Personal Life
Retreat from Intimacy

*She is a sophomore, wearing her baseball cap, the
1990s equivalent of the tie-dyed T-shirt, backwards.
At her feet is a backpack, and she is holding a water
bottle. Her clothes are loose and baggy. She looks like
an ad for the Gap. When we ask her what she does
for fun, she tells us, "Sleep."*

*He is wearing a business suit and two earrings. He
tells us he likes to go to clubs for fun. On his campus,
"Everyone drinks. They drink to get drunk."*

*She is wearing Spandex and he's wearing long shorts.
They say there is "no dating" on campus. Both agree
intimate relationships are frightening. They have
never seen a successful adult romantic relationship.*

Fear and Pain

Today's students are frightened. They are afraid of getting hurt.
Nearly half of all undergraduates (46 percent) worry about becoming victims of violent crime. Among women the proportion is even
higher (54 percent) (Undergraduate Survey, 1993). We asked a
female junior on a suburban campus in an affluent area why she was

afraid. She could not think of any incidents that had occurred on her campus. Instead, she told us the college had recently introduced emergency phones, stronger outdoor lighting, and nighttime escort services. For her, cause and prevention were the same thing. Both fueled her fears.

Students were also frightened about their economic prospects. Many have had financially unstable lives. More than one-fifth (21 percent) of the undergraduates surveyed reported the ultimate instability: someone who helped pay their tuition had been unemployed during their college years (Undergraduate Survey, 1993). The students saw their own economic futures as uncertain too. They told us over and over again that they were worried about whether they could pay their college tuition. In an age in which students are taking average loans of $3,210 per year at two-year colleges and $4,790 per year at four-year colleges (U.S. Department of Education, 1996c), three college students out of every ten are uncertain whether they have enough money to complete college; this is more than a 50 percent increase since 1976. In fact, only 25 percent of undergraduates were confident of having sufficient funds to pay for college (Table 5.1). They were equally frightened about whether they would be able to repay their college loans, whether they could find a decent job after college, and whether they could afford a home and a family—or would have to move back home with their parents.

Table 5.1. Student concern about ability to finance a college education: 1976, 1993.

Financial concern	Percentage reporting	
	1976	1993
Confident they will have sufficient funds	38	25
Probably will have enough funds	43	45
Not sure they will have enough funds to complete college	19	30

Source: Undergraduate Surveys (1976, 1993).

Relationships were another source of concern for students. Nearly one-third of all college freshmen (30 percent) grew up with one or no parent (Sax, Astin, Korn, and Mahoney, 1996). Even those students who lived with both parents usually experienced divorce up close by seeing it in the lives of their friends and neighbors. These students often told us of unhappy relationships between their own parents. The result is that current undergraduates worry a great deal about divorce. As one dean of students put it: "They want a nurturing and caring environment. They want security. They don't want divorce to happen to them." They are desperate to have only one marriage, and they want it to be happy. They don't know whether this is possible anymore.

Again and again, deans of students reported on the growing rate of dysfunctional families among their students. They talked of violence; instability; blended families; and emotional, sexual, and financial problems. As one dean put it, "It's hard to send a student home, when home is the problem."

In interviews, students alluded to such difficulties, often very subtly. Others were more concrete, particularly in regard to the feeling of not having a home. Startlingly, 27 percent of the students surveyed had moved four or more times while growing up; 16 percent had moved more than five times. Among students of color, the proportions were even higher, 36 percent and 20 percent respectively (Undergraduate Survey, 1993). For these students, there were frequently no roots, no sense of place, and no strong relationships. They yearned deeply for all of these things but feared they would never have them.

The bottom line is that students are coming to college overwhelmed and more damaged than those of previous years. Six out of ten chief student affairs officers (60 percent) reported that undergraduates are using psychological counseling services in record numbers and for longer periods of time than in the past; this is true at 69 percent of four-year schools and 52 percent of two-year colleges. Eating disorders are up at 58 percent of the institutions surveyed.

Classroom disruption increased at a startling 44 percent of colleges, drug abuse at 42 percent, alcohol abuse at 35 percent of campuses. Gambling has grown at 25 percent of the institutions, and suicide attempts have risen at 23 percent (Student Affairs Survey, 1997). Deans of students concluded:

"Students carry more baggage to college today."

"Dealing with more developmentally delayed or disabled students."

"Much more time devoted to emotionally-ill students."

"We deal with a greater number of dysfunctional students and dysfunctional family situations."

"Dealing with more psychopathology among students of all levels and all backgrounds."

"Students bring more nonacademic-related issues. We are becoming a secondary social service agency."

"I spend more time dealing with student discipline, stalking, harassment, and domestic violence."

"Students expect the community to respond to their needs— to make 'right' their personal problems and those of society at large." (Student Affairs Survey, 1997)

The effect of the accumulated fears and hurts that students have experienced is to divide and isolate them. Undergraduates have developed a lifeboat mentality of sorts. It is as if each student is alone in a boat in a terrible storm, far from any harbor. The boat is taking on water and believed to be in imminent danger of sinking. Under these circumstances, there is but one alternative: each student must single-mindedly bail. Conditions are so bad that no one has time to care for others who may also be foundering. No distractions are permitted. The pressure is enormous and unremitting.

This situation has resulted in a generation often too busy or too tired to have a social life. It has produced students who fear intimacy in relationships. Withdrawal is easier and less dangerous than engagement. It has led to undergraduates who want things to be different; escaping from the campus physically and from life via a bottle are both popular.

Social life is an area in which student fears loom larger than their hopes. Their behavior differs in this realm from that in the political arena. Though fears and doubts about politics, politicians, and government are extremely high, students have chosen to engage, albeit through the local and more informal approach of community service. In part, the reason stated for their involvement is that they had no choice; they had to embrace the political agenda or it would engulf them. In contrast, a social life is viewed by undergraduates as optional. To be intimately involved is a higher-stakes game than politics. It presents a far greater potential for getting hurt, for adding to one's burden, or for personal failure.

Having Fun?

We asked students what they did for fun. We had asked the same question in the prior study, but this time the answers were very different (Table 5.2).

We also asked the same question of deans of students, who responded similarly regarding the most popular activities but tended to give greater preference to more wholesome pursuits (Table 5.3).

With many students, the question drew a wide-eyed stare or a look of bemusement, as if to ask the interviewer, What are you talking about? What planet do you come from? On nearly one-third of the campuses (30 percent) at which we conducted focus group interviews, students said they had no social life. This is only a small increase (27 percent) from the earlier study, but for the first time students (11 percent) listed "sleeping" as a form of recreation. The students at the University of Colorado who selected "tired" as the best adjective to describe their generation apparently knew what they were talking about.

Table 5.2. What college students do for fun, according to students: 1979, 1993.

Activities	Percentage of students reporting	
	1979	1993
Drinking	77	63
Clubs and bars	—	59
Off-campus	—	52
Parties	38	41
Sports and intramurals	54	33
No social life, commuter	27	30
Theater	—	26
Music	27	22
Movies	27	22
Concerts	12	22
Fraternities and sororities	19	15
Study	—	21
Travel and trips	8	11
Dances	58	11
Drugs	54	[a]
Sleep	—	11
Residence hall activities	19	—
Cards, backgammon	12	—
Running	12	—

[a]Students talked about drugs regularly, but most often in the negative, saying drug use on campus was less popular than alcohol use.

Source: Campus Site Visits (1979, 1993).

Table 5.3. What students do for fun, according
to deans of students: 1997.

| | Percentage of deans reporting | | |
Activities	Two-year schools	Four-year schools	Total
Party	17	52	34
Sports	48	51	50
Drink	9	50	29
Socialize	39	36	37
Games	30	15	23
Video	13	30	21
Outdoor	13	24	18
Comedy or other entertainment	22	7	15
Clubs	13	16	14
Music	9	15	12
Greek	—	9	5
Date	—	2	7

Source: Student Affairs Survey (1997).

Studying was another leisure activity making a first-time appearance on the fun list. It was cited on more than one-fifth of the campuses (21 percent). Undergraduates told us again and again:

"I don't have a social life."

"There is no free time."

"My whole life is juggling."

"Study, that's all we ever do."

"I'm always behind. I never catch up."

"I feel run down."

"People's lives are dictated by their jobs."

"The high cost means I have to work forty to fifty hours per week, and it's killing me. Sometimes I fall asleep in class."

For many undergraduates, "life is just work, school, and home." There may be time to gulp the coffee, but there is absolutely "no time to smell the coffee." This is no surprise given the dramatic rise in the proportion of students who work while attending college (now about 60 percent) or the growing percentage who are working full-time (currently 24 percent overall and as high as 39 percent at two-year colleges) (Undergraduate Survey, 1993). During the 1990s, 71 percent of the colleges surveyed reported increases in the proportion of students working while attending college (Student Affairs Survey, 1997). The increase in part-time attenders and students with families is also a factor. Today almost one in five college students (18 percent) has dependent children (Undergraduate Survey, 1993). With all the demands on their time, something has got to give. They have elected to sacrifice social life.

But not all of the retreat from social life is time-based. Chief student affairs officers described students more often as loners than in the past. Requests for single dormitory rooms have skyrocketed. The thought of having a roommate is less appealing than it once was. Perhaps this desire to withdraw simply mirrors the national trend of disengagement from groups that once connected individuals with a broad swath of other people who shared similar interests. Across the country we are losing our "social capital"—the networks and norms of society—as civic organizations once as commonplace and popular as the Boy Scouts and local bowling leagues have suffered huge declines in membership; so laments Robert Putnam in his thought-provoking essay "Bowling Alone" (1995).

Similarly, group activities that once connected students on college campuses are losing their appeal and are becoming more individualized. For instance, the venue for television watching has moved from the lounge to the dorm room. Film viewing has shifted from the theater to the home VCR. As one student put it, these days dormitory rooms come "fully loaded." A dean of students said he was worried about wiring; can it support the electronic menagerie behind each residence hall door? Equally important is whether colleges can afford to support financially the needed upgrades in wiring, cable, and other technological infrastructure demanded and expected by current undergraduates. Student rooms have microwaves, televisions, VCRs, computers, CD players, tape decks, phones, answering machines, refrigerators, coffee makers, and who knows what else. The dean said, "Everything is right there." He could not imagine a reason, other than eating or attending class, why a student would need to leave his or her room.

That is the point. Increasingly, students are living their lives in ways that allow them not to venture out.

Social Life Moves Off Campus

None of this is to say that collegiate social life is dead, but it is moving off campus. In 1979, on-campus activities topped the list of what students did for fun. They attended dances, they participated in intramurals, and they went to parties. There were also movies, music, Greek life, dormitory activities, and cards. With the exception of parties, every one of these activities declined in popularity in the recent survey. Dances, particularly on-campus events, plummeted, dropping by a factor of five. Intramurals, though still a staple of campus life, declined in favor by nearly 40 percent. Residence hall activities and card playing fell off the charts (see Table 5.1). Participation in Greek life (fraternities and sororities) declined by 43 percent. Between 1986 and 1992, the proportion of undergraduates involved in Greek organizations fell from 4.4 percent to 2.5 percent (Center for the Study of the College Fraternity, 1992). And during the 1990s, interest in fraternities and sororities declined at 43 percent of the nation's four-year colleges (Student Affairs Survey, 1997).

Today, there is probably a greater diversity of on-campus activities available than ever before, but each activity, in the words of the chief student affairs officer of the University of Southern Mississippi, "appeals to smaller pockets of students." This is, in many respects, the consequence of student organizational mitosis and the multi-plication of the divides between undergraduates. Deans of students regularly told us: "There is less larger group socializing," "Groups have become more specialized and so have their activities," and "More people are doing things individually and in separate groups than campuswide" (Student Affairs Survey, 1997).

This is particularly apparent in terms of the speakers who are most popular today. In the 1978 study, entertainers topped the list and drew crowds from across the campus. Today, deans say it is harder to draw a big crowd. Most popular are "niche speakers," decidedly ethnic and of color, appealing to particular campus pop-ulations; they include Colin Powell, Elie Wiesel, Cornel West, Greg Louganis, Jesse Jackson, Joycelyn Elders, the Reverend Al Sharp-ton, Spike Lee, and Danny Glover. They are social activists, focus-ing on critical social issues. By any stretch of the imagination, only Colin Powell and Jesse Jackson could be thought of as establishment figures (Student Affairs Survey, 1997).

In the main, students are leaving campus to have fun. At more than half of the colleges we visited (52 percent), students didn't bother to mention a specific activity or locale when they talked about what they did for fun; they said they just "go off campus." When they did get more specific, clubs and bars were the location of choice (59 percent), referred to by a student at Manhattan Col-lege as the "main social outpost." The club-and-bar scene is a new addition to the list. Although students mentioned bars and clubs infrequently in the 1979 study, these places have exploded as a response in the current survey, topping the list as the locale where college students most often go to have fun. Also rising on the list is travel and trips, and such on-campus and off-campus activities as concerts and theater.

These changes in student answers are not particularly shocking, either. In fact, only 30 percent of all college students live on cam-pus. The proportion has dropped by one-third since the late 1960s, while the percentage living in off-campus housing has more than tripled (Table 5.4).

Table 5.4. Undergraduate living arrangements during most recent college term: 1969, 1976, 1993.

Living arrangements	Percentage of students reporting		
	1969	1976	1993
Apartment or house (not parents')	12	34	39
College housing	44	30	30
Parents' or other relatives' home	32	28	25
Rooming house or rented room	3	2	3
Fraternity or sorority house	4	2	2
Other	4	5	3

Source: Undergraduate Surveys (1969, 1976, 1993).

A 1991 survey by the Higher Education Research Institute at the University of California, Los Angeles, found that only 44 percent of college students who lived in residence halls as freshmen continued to reside there as seniors (Higher Education Research Institute, 1992). Add to this the fact that students are also spending less time on campus owing to jobs and part-time attendance, and the result is that increasingly campuses are places in which instruction is the principal activity. Living and social life occur elsewhere. In this vein, on many campuses with low residential populations, the library is becoming a center of activity for students. Over the past five years, 57 percent of colleges and universities surveyed reported increased student library usage. This is much more the case, for instance, at two-year (67 percent) than at four-year (45 percent) colleges (Student Affairs Survey, 1997).

Drinking, the Great Escape

College students say the number one fun-time activity for them is drinking. This was true in 1979 too. Cigarette smoking and marijuana use are on the rise on campus as well. The Harvard School of Public Health reports that nearly one-third (32 percent) of college students have smoked within the past year, while 25 percent have used some kind of illegal drug over the same time period (Wechsler, 1996). Similar findings were revealed in national research at the Core Institute at Southern Illinois University in Carbondale and the University of Michigan Institute for Social Research (Presley, Meilman, and Lyerla, 1995; *World Almanac and Book of Facts*, 1997). Marijuana was used by 24 percent of college students, cocaine by 4 percent, and hallucinogens by nearly 5 percent (Presley, Meilman, and Lyerla, 1995).

In general, students dismissed cigarette smoking (in spite of their behavior) as "dumb." Few students we asked thought they would still be smoking in twenty years. At the moment, they felt young and invulnerable. Still, 38 percent of colleges and universities surveyed reported increases in student smoking during the 1990s. The rise was greater at four-year colleges (50 percent) than at two-year schools (27 percent) (Student Affairs Survey, 1997).

Undergraduates spoke about drugs differently. Their attitude seemed to be not so much that drugs were good or bad, as that they were unimportant and peripheral to their lives. Even so, 42 percent of deans of students said drug abuse was increasing on their campuses (Student Affairs Survey, 1997). At most institutions, students said there were drugs on campus, but they were not a staple:

"Only crunchy types do marijuana."

"Taking drugs is not an 'in' thing in the nineties."

"It is more an individual than a group thing."

"Drugs are not cool."

"The drug culture here is very hidden. When I was in high school, I knew where to go to get drugs."

"[It's] not like the sixties."

Drugs were just not a big deal to students. This represents a sharp contrast with their younger brothers and sisters, aged twelve to seventeen, for whom drug use is rising—141 percent between 1992 and 1995 (Goldberg, 1996). They will be coming to college soon.

Attitudes about drinking were dramatically different. Here's what students from coast to coast, at all types of colleges and universities, told us:

"Drugs are looked down on, but drinking is not."

"Alcohol is big."

"Alcohol is very popular."

"Alcohol is the drug of choice."

"Drinking is a big part of life here."

"There is a lot of drinking."

"Everyone drinks."

"People here drink to get drunk."

"Without beer it's not a party."

Nationwide, 84 percent of college students reported having drunk alcohol within the last year (Wechsler, 1996). This is a notable proportion, considering that drinking is as a rule illegal for people under the age of twenty-one. In any case, legal or illegal, alcohol and college have always gone together. Indeed, in 1639, the first college president in this country (at colonial Harvard) was fired in part because his wife was said to be watering down the students' beer, which was served routinely with meals (Morison, [1936] 1964).

Perhaps more important than the pervasiveness of alcohol on campus is the amount students are drinking. We met students who told us they never drank because they disapproved of drinking on religious grounds, for health reasons, owing to the cost, or because of having alcoholic relatives. Or they simply disliked the taste of alcohol or didn't enjoy what drinking did to them. These students are the exception. Light drinking has actually declined on college campuses over the past decade (Hanson and Engs, 1992; Wechsler, Isaac, Grodstein, and Sellers, 1994). In contrast, binge drinking—consuming five or more drinks in succession for men, four for women—is booming. A national survey by the Harvard School of Public Health (Wechsler, 1996) found that 44 percent of college students who drink have binged within the last two weeks. Even more staggering, nearly one-fifth of all college students (19 percent) are frequent binge drinkers, in this case defined by Wechsler as those who have binged three or more times in the previous two weeks.

The research found, too, that binge rates varied greatly from institution to institution, ranging from as little as 1 percent of the student population to as much as 70 percent. This variation was a result of a number of factors, including the culture and traditions of the institution, its geographic location in the country, and whether it was primarily a residential or a commuter school (Wechsler, 1996).

The effects of college student drinking are being felt profoundly on campus. According to the Commission on Substance Abuse at Colleges and Universities:

- In the last five years the number of emergency admissions for alcohol poisoning on college campuses has risen 15 percent.

- Sixty percent of college women diagnosed last year with a sexually transmitted disease were drunk at the time of infection.

- Two-thirds of college student suicide victims were intoxicated at the time of death.

- Alcohol is involved in 80 percent of campus vandalism, 90 percent of campus rapes, and 95 percent of violent crime on campus (1994, p. 4).

More routinely, the consequences are missing classes, hangovers, and getting behind in school work. Even more serious are unplanned or unprotected sexual activity, getting hurt physically, hurting someone else, and doing something the student regretted later (Table 5.5). If a student falls victim to a mixture of alcohol with the illegal, extremely potent, and increasingly popular "date rape" drug Rohypnol, the effects can be far worse (Smith, Wesson, and Calhoun, 1997).

Student affairs officers and students themselves confirmed this state of affairs on our nation's campuses. "More kids drink every day," observed the dean at the University of Colorado. "They stagger from party to party." An upperclass woman at Drake University targeted the freshmen, in particular, as problem drinkers. "Their philosophy is that you are not drunk enough if you still remember," she commented wryly.

Table 5.5. Percentage of college drinkers
reporting alcohol-related problems: 1996.

Problems experienced in connection with alcohol use	Non-binge drinkers	Bingers	Frequent bingers
Had a hangover	30	75	90
Did something they regretted later	14	37	63
Missed a class	8	30	61
Forgot where they were or what they did	8	26	54
Got behind in school work	6	21	46
Argued with friends	8	22	42
Engaged in unplanned sexual activity	8	20	41
Had unprotected sex	4	10	22
Got hurt or injured	2	9	23
Damaged property	2	8	22
Got into trouble with campus or local police	1	4	11
Required treatment for alcohol overdose	<1	<1	1

Source: Wechsler (1996, p. 23).

Students, whether they drank or not, often complained about the problems that drinking by others caused them. They spoke of unwanted sexual advances, loss of sleep, property damage, inability to study, and aggressive behavior (Table 5.6).

We asked students when they drank: "anytime" and "all the time" were not entirely uncommon responses. But the more typical answer was "weekends," defined by a student at Catholic University and many of her peers around the country as "Thursday through Sunday." These are the party nights: "We do homework from 7:00 P.M. to 11:00 P.M. and then go out."

We also asked students why they drank. They gave a variety of answers: "due to type A-ness," said an Oglethorpe University student; "because of stress," responded an undergraduate at the Illinois Institute of Technology. Still another, at the University of Northern Iowa, explained: "People drink to relax. A lot of people drink to get drunk. They think they can express themselves. With alcohol they feel they can be honest." We heard scores of explanations of why students drink. What they added up to is that they do it to escape.

Table 5.6. Percentage of students at low-binge and high-binge institutions reporting secondhand alcohol-related problems: 1996.

Campus problems due to others' drinking	Low-binge	High-binge
Was insulted or humiliated	21	34
Experienced unwanted sexual advances (data from women's responses only)	15	26
Had a serious argument or quarrel	13	20
Was pushed, hit, or assaulted	7	13
Studying or sleep was interrupted	42	68
Had to "baby-sit" a drunken student	31	54
Personal property was damaged	6	15
Suffered sexual assault or "date rape"	2	2

Source: Wechsler (1996, p. 60).

Retreat from Intimacy

One of the things undergraduates have been most eager to escape from is intimate relationships. Traditional dating is largely dead on college campuses. At institutions all around the country, students told us, in the words of a University of Colorado undergraduate, "There is no such thing as dating here."

Two-person dating has been replaced by group dating, in which men and women travel in unpartnered packs. It's a practice that provides protection from deeper involvement and intimacy. "Large groups are seen as low risk, making for a safer emotional environment," explained a student at the University of Northern Iowa. Besides, "it's not cool to be in a dating relationship," added the dean at Rollins College.

Of course, there are exceptions. At Catholic University, the dean of students talked about the very small number of couples who meet during the first days of college and go everywhere and do everything together. They are joined at the hip. "Velcro buddies," she called them.

At a few schools, relationships were considered more acceptable by older students. As a woman at Drake University explained, the diversity of students on campuses today means "people are in different life stages. The seniors are more into relationships." A student at Southern Methodist echoed her sentiments and summed up the dating scene this way: "I don't think there is much serious dating until people are seniors. I mean, people go out a lot but do not want serious relationships. There is a lot of sex. College is about casual sex."

Students talked a lot about sex. In marked contrast with the earlier study, they commonly told us intimate details about their sex lives. One student at Boston University cried and admitted she was a virgin.

Students used a special vocabulary to describe sexual relations, including terms such as scoping, clocking, hooking, scamming, scrumping, mashing, and shacking. The particular terms used and their definitions varied from college to college, as indicated in the glossary below. In any case, neither the terms nor their meanings were romantic. They were largely devoid of emotional content.

A Sexual Glossary with Student Definitions

Scoping

"Guys checking out girls."

"Just looking."

"Sizing up the room, especially at parties."

Clocking

"Guys rating girls, and vice versa."

Hooking or Hooking Up

"Informal dating, as in hooking up."

"Getting together. It can be for sex. It can also be for just a date."

"One-night stand, nothing after that."

Scamming

"Running a game on someone."

"Watching—you know, elevator eyes."

"Checking out members of the opposite sex. If you're lucky, you end up in bed."

"Hitting on someone. Sometimes it is just to get to know them."

"Group dating leading to sex after drinking."

"Trying to get girls to go to bed."

"Going to a party with the intention of meeting up with somebody, though not necessarily sexually, especially for women. But men always have sex on their mind."

Scrumping

"Another term for sex."

Mashing

"A sexual encounter."

Shacking

"Staying in someone's room at night but not necessarily sleeping with them—a PC word."

"People go out in a group to scope, then scam, then shack."

Call it "hooking," "scamming," or what you will, the alternative to traditional dating is developing a sexual relationship that is not intended to be emotional. On a given night, the typical pattern is to go to a bar or party off campus, get drunk, and end up back in someone's room. A student at the University of the District of Columbia explained, "People will stand in the bar just waiting to be taken at the end of the night." Sex was described largely as a succession of one-night stands fueled by alcohol. Several colleges had a "walk of shame," the path a woman (never a man) had to follow back to the residence hall the morning after. As a student at the University of Northern Iowa put it, "People don't talk about . . . sex; they just do it." Perhaps this is unavoidable, given the gender gap described in Chapter Four.

Gender was a topic students did not discuss. Like race, it was too hard. The stresses were too great. As a group of women at Wellesley explained it, their inner struggle is to deal with the conflict between their political agenda—getting ahead and, therefore, "feeling more antimale"—and their personal agenda, which is to build heterosexual relationships. The difficulty lies in the attempt to reconcile the two.

Males were neither as eloquent nor as thoughtful in describing gender differences. In the main, it was simply not on the male radar screen. In fact, there was a marked contrast between male discussions of gender and sexuality. Conversation abounded on sexuality; gender brought scant discussion.

Women were sometimes described as "angry." The word "feminazi" was used periodically. (Incidentally, the word "feminist" was thought to have negative connotations by both men and women; it was too strident and "too dated.") There was talk of not understanding women: "They talk a different language"; "they think different[ly]." Men spoke of pressures from peers. "I supported the ERA [Equal Rights Amendment] and got called a 'fag' for doing it. This campus is not supportive of men who want to support women," sadly reported a student at Northern Iowa University. There was discussion of the threats men felt from women in the workplace and the classroom. At the University of Texas at Arlington, the dean observed, "I see a lot of trauma, especially for young white men. Women and minorities are challenging the shrinking job pool. Men find a macho conviviality in alcohol, and this leads to angry feelings and abuse, especially sexual abuse." Fifty-five percent of the institutions surveyed had increases in sexual harassment reports, and 41 percent experienced rises in acquaintance rape and sexual assault reports (Student Affairs Survey, 1997). There was also sympathy and support from men regarding glass ceilings and discrimination against women.

In the main, students have decided to ignore their gender differences and the tensions between them. The easiest way to accomplish this has been to squeeze romance and emotion from sexual relationships. There has been a propensity under these circumstances to trade quality for quantity.

This is a very dangerous decision in an age of AIDS. But condoms appear to be nearly omnipresent on college campuses. They can be obtained in residence halls and fraternity houses, in restrooms and laundry rooms, in health centers and student unions. At Los Angeles Valley College, a condom was tucked into a fanny pack around the waist of a teddy bear for sale at a dance-a-thon to support AIDS victims. At Catholic University, condoms were slipped into copies of the student newspaper. In fraternity houses at Georgia Tech, there is a KOC, the Keeper of Condoms, to keep men supplied. Do they get used? Who knows? However, students on several campuses, including Wellesley, Berkshire Community College in Massachusetts, and the University of Texas at Arlington, told us bowls of free condoms get emptied every day.

Although almost all students (91 percent) said they are well informed about what constitutes "safe sex," under half of those who are sexually active (49 percent) said they always practiced it. Another fifth say they sometimes practice safe sex (Undergraduate Survey, 1993). Campus interviews with both chief student affairs officers and undergraduates themselves reveal a limited student understanding of safe sex, ambiguity about the dividing line between health risks and issues of morality, and a sense of almost complete invincibility. The dean at Concordia College in Oregon observed, "I think twelve-to-twenty-two-year-olds still feel indestructible."

On our site visits, students offered comments of their own. "The thinking here is that sex is fairly safe—that nice white kids don't get AIDS," noted a student at Carleton. Others said students are talking about it or are choosing partners more carefully. A sophomore at Los Angeles Valley College laughed when we asked if people's patterns of behavior had changed. "Last year we ran a survey," he replied. "The majority said they have changed in practice, but they also said they have not changed in the number of partners they have. Most said five or more." When questioned about the effect of AIDS on her campus, a student at Boston University replied, "I think AIDS means you look at people differently, that you observe them for a while." Of course, a number of students suggested the waiting period was until the second "date."

A student at the Illinois Institute of Technology put it all into perspective. He said, "I'm more afraid of getting shot on the way home than of getting AIDS." He was scared and he was angry. He was worried about getting hurt both in his neighborhood and in his personal relationships. He wanted things to be different. As a fellow student put it, "We're further and further away from the college life our parents had."

Of course, current students may be envisioning a collegiate life far more romantic than the one their parents actually experienced. It, too, was beset by personal fears and campus tensions—gender and racial gaps, campus violence, substance abuse, the restrictive doctrine of *in loco parentis*, and a Vietnam draft. However, today's undergraduates are genuinely burdened by their own set of issues and live a life the previous generation could not have imagined. They worry about relationships, crime, financing a college education, AIDS, and their economic prospects for the future. They come to college more damaged psychologically, and they socialize differently, often alone or away from campus. Binge drinking, which frequently mixes with sex, is on the rise, but traditional dating has all but disappeared. More work at jobs and live off campus, which contributes to their social isolation. Although their ways of having fun are much the same as those of their parents—parties, sports, music, movies, and watching TV—many are too exhausted to think beyond the demands of work, relationships, and school. These very same pressures are remarkable and apparent in their academic life as well.

6

• •

Academics

Search for an Insurance Policy

*"Academics are a means to an end. There is no
emphasis on learning for its own sake."*
        Student, Georgia Tech

In the late 1970s, student affairs officers were asked how undergraduates had changed since the 1960s. At the top of their list,
71 percent said students were more career oriented (Student Affairs
Survey, 1978). The career orientation is even more pronounced
today. Students want job security, and three-quarters of them want to
be very well off financially (Undergraduate Survey, 1993). Although
they do not believe a college education provides a money-back guarantee of future success, they feel it is not possible to obtain a good job
without one, much less a lucrative or prestigious job. At the very
least, it is a kind of insurance policy to hedge bets against the future.
As a student at Portland Community College put it, "College is the
difference between white-collar and blue-collar work." Fifty-seven
percent of undergraduates believe that the chief benefit of a college
education is increasing one's earning power, an 11-percentage-point
increase since 1976 (Undergraduate Surveys, 1976, 1993).

Why Go to College?

By far the most important reason students say they go to college in
the 1990s is to prepare for a career. "Task-oriented students who

focus on jobs" is how Georgia Tech's vice president for student affairs labeled them. "Their minds are focused on fulfilling goals," agreed the dean at nearby Morris Brown College in Atlanta.

Indeed, by the time they reach college, 85 percent of students report they have come with a specific career in mind. More than one-third (37 percent) admit that, if they thought attending college wasn't helping their job chances, they would drop out (Undergraduate Survey, 1993).

As Table 6.1 shows, mastery of a specific field and training for an occupation far outdistance all other benefits considered essential in a college education (Undergraduate Survey, 1993).

Financial reward is seen as the big payoff. Data from the Higher Education Research Institute confirm this vocational leaning. In 1996, 77 percent of the freshmen surveyed singled out getting a better job as the most important reason to go to college. Seventy-two percent said they went in order to make more money, an 18-percentage-point increase since 1976 (Astin, Parrott, Korn, and Sax, 1997).

Even more dramatic than this continuing trend toward vocationalism, however, is the plummeting value placed on nonmaterial goals, such as learning to get along with people and formulating the values and goals of one's life. Whereas these personal and philosophic goals were the principal reasons for attending college in the 1960s, today they are at the bottom of the list.

This basic pattern holds across all groups of students, whatever their age, race, gender, full-time or part-time attendance status, or the type of institution they attend. Although different subgroups vary widely in terms of how they rate other advantages of a college education, they think alike on the importance of career benefits.

This should not come as any surprise. As mentioned in Chapter Five, the anxiety resulting from the belief that jobs are not secure in today's economy has deeply affected college students. Since three-quarters of Americans know someone who has lost a job (Sanger, 1996), it is perfectly reasonable for most students to

Table 6.1. What undergraduates feel it is essential to get from a college education: 1969, 1976, 1993.

Benefits of a college education	Percentage of undergraduates saying essential			Change since 1969	Change since 1976
	1969	1976	1993		
Detailed grasp of a special field	62	68	71	+9	+3
Training and skills for an occupation	59	67	70	+11	+3
Well-rounded general education	57	57	57	0	0
Formulating the values and goals of my life	71	62	50	−21	−12
Learning to get along with people	76	66	47	−29	−19

Source: Undergraduate Surveys (1969, 1976, 1993).

translate that knowledge into concern for their own futures and preparation for a career, like the student at Drake who said, "I know too many people who have a college degree and no job." Furthermore, the need for so many students to work while attending college (60 percent) and even work full-time while in attendance (24 percent) results in a very purposeful, career-oriented mind-set about the undergraduate experience (Undergraduate Survey, 1993). Students in the latter group don't work their way through college; rather, they work college into their lives. For almost all students who hold jobs, whether employed twenty or forty hours a week, the notion of college as a place to luxuriate in close friendships and lose oneself in philosophic reflection is a relic of a bygone era.

Women students seem to be taking the employment situation most seriously. They are more likely than men to complete a bachelor's degree (49 percent versus 43 percent), no matter how long it takes them to finish. In addition to endurance, they demonstrate speed: they're more likely to graduate earlier than men, 43 percent in four years versus 37 percent (Astin, Tsui, and Avalos, 1996). Furthermore, they have been actively investing in additional job insurance by undertaking graduate and professional degree work. Since 1984, their numbers have exceeded those of men in graduate school; by 1994 there were 21 percent more women than men enrolled at this level. Between 1984 and 1994, the growth rate for women has been more than two times that of men for full-time students, and nearly four times that of men for part-time study (U.S. Department of Education, 1996b).

Not only have women raised their sights, but the educational degree goals for all students have risen in the past twenty years. To all intents and purposes, the master's degree has replaced the bachelor's in the minds of students as the entry-level credential for professional jobs. The result is a sizable drop in the number of freshmen planning to end their formal education at the bachelor's level and an increase in those aiming for a master's, doctoral, or professional degree, as shown in Table 6.2.

Table 6.2. Highest degree planned, by gender: 1976, 1996.

Degree aspirations	Percentage of freshmen planning					
	All freshmen		Men		Women	
	1976	1996	1976	1996	1976	1996
None	3	1	3	1	3	1
Vocational or equivalent	—	1	—	1	—	1
Associate degree	8	4	7	3	10	4
Bachelor's degree	36	26	34	28	37	25
Master's degree	29	39	28	38	29	39
Ph.D. or Ed.D.	9	15	10	15	8	15
M.D., D.D.S., D.V.M., or D.O.	7	9	8	8	6	10
L.L. or J.D. (law)	5	4	6	4	4	4
B.D. or M.Div. (divinity)	1	<1	1	1	<1	<1
Other	3	2	3	2	3	2

Source: Data from Astin, Parrott, Korn, and Sax (1997).

Such aspirations are not merely the dreams of idealistic fresh-men, though achievement has lagged behind hopes historically. As students become upperclassmen and graduates, these dreams are coming true. In the ten-year period between 1984 and 1994, the National Center for Education Statistics recorded a 36 percent increase in the number of master's degrees and a 30 percent increase in doctoral degrees awarded (U.S. Department of Education, 1996b). During the same period the proportion of students taking the Graduate Record Examination for admission to graduate school has risen steadily. This rate peaked in 1992, when 36 percent of all seniors were taking the test. This is 1 percentage point higher than 1971, during the Vietnam War, when graduate school attendance provided a college deferment and test taking was sky high (U.S. Department of Education, 1996b).

Enrollment patterns also reflect students' vocational orientation, which, among other things, is driving the choice of their major or area of concentration. As Table 6.3 shows, majors with a vocational emphasis (when combined) are attracting about 60 percent of all students. The big winners are business, education, and the health professions, fields where the occupational opportunities are promising and the job insurance protection is better than average.

In support of these aspirations, undergraduates are forming pre-professional clubs in career areas such as business, engineering, and law. These campus clubs are skyrocketing, both in number and in the percentage of undergraduates who participate in them. They can be found on more than three-quarters (78 percent) of all college campuses and are the largest and most popular student organizations on campus today, according to the student affairs officers surveyed. Indeed, 40 percent of student affairs deans cited them as the most popular groups at their schools (Student Affairs Surveys, 1992, 1997).

Yet, despite the occupational orientation and material preoccupation that predominate among students, there are some indications that the curricular pendulum may have swung as far as it is going to

Table 6.3. Bachelor's degrees awarded by field of study: 1975–76, 1985–86, and 1993–94.

	Number of degrees awarded and percentage of change				
Academic field	1975–76	1985–86	Percent change, 1975–76 to 1985–86	1993–94	Percent change, 1985–86 to 1993–94
Architecture and related programs	9,146	9,119	0	8,975	–2
Agriculture and natural resources	19,402	16,823	–13	18,070	+7
Biological and life sciences	54,275	38,524	–29	51,383	+33
Business management	142,034	237,319	+67	246,654	+4
Communications	20,045	41,666	+108	51,164	+23
Computer and information sciences	5,652	41,889	+641	24,200	–42
Education	154,437	87,114	–44	107,600	+24
Engineering	38,388	76,225	+99	62,220	–18
Engineering-related technologies	7,943	19,435	+145	16,005	–18
English language and literature	42,006	34,552	–18	53,924	+56
Foreign languages and literature	16,484	10,984	–33	14,378	+31
Health professions	53,958	64,396	+19	74,424	+16
Liberal studies	18,855	21,336	+13	33,397	+57
Mathematics	16,329	17,147	+5	14,396	–16
Multidisciplinary or interdisciplinary studies	13,588	13,489	–1	25,167	+87
Philosophy and religion	8,447	6,239	–26	7,546	+21
Physical sciences	21,465	21,717	+1	18,400	–15
Psychology	50,278	40,628	–19	69,259	+70
Public administration	15,440	11,887	–23	17,815	+50
Social sciences and history	126,396	93,840	–26	133,680	+42
Visual and performing arts	42,138	37,241	–12	49,053	+32

Source: U.S. Department of Education, 1996b, p. 274.

go. After a multiyear gain, majors in business are leveling off. Compared to an increase of 67 percent between 1976 and 1986, these majors increased only an additional 4 percent through 1994. Majors in engineering dropped 18 percent between 1986 and 1994, while computer and information sciences decreased a dramatic 42 percent. At the same time, less vocationally oriented liberal arts fields in English literature and psychology are enjoying a rather substantial surge in popularity, up 56 percent and 70 percent respectively (U.S. Department of Education, 1996b).

Students are also asking for "relevance" in their studies. This is not relevance in the 1960s sense of "let's tie-dye T-shirts together." Rather, undergraduates see the whole world around them changing. They want their curriculum to be updated and to discuss the changes. As a junior at UC, Santa Barbara, told us, "Faculty can't just keep teaching the same old things. The whole world is changing. They can't ignore this." In part, this is a reflection of rising student social activism.

Academic Climate

When we asked students at the site visit campuses how seriously their classmates take academics, we received almost as many answers as we did to our question about ways of having fun. Once again, there were no surprises. The degree to which academics are taken seriously varies by institution, by the student body, even by the time of the year. We were told the following:

> "About half of the students don't care. The other half *really* care. They're receiving honors and are very involved. Nontraditional students take education seriously: they're here for themselves."
> —Berkshire Community College

> "In the freshman and sophomore years, students just get by and are more interested in meeting people than taking the academics seriously. The exceptions are the freshmen and sophomores who know what they're going to do."
> —University of Minnesota

"The younger students act like this is an extension of high school."
—Portland Community College

"When you pay for it yourself, you take it seriously."
—Concordia College

"The hard majors like economics and accounting are taken seriously. Teaching as a major is a joke."
—University of Northern Iowa

"Minorities take academics seriously. It's a struggle."
—Manhattan College

"Most students take academics seriously. By spring, though, they're fed up. They've learned some tricks."
—Illinois Institute of Technology

"Students take academics too seriously. Stress runs rampant."
—Wellesley College

"People take both studying and going out seriously."
—Catholic University

"There's a progression over the four years from working hard to being intellectual and to figuring out what it all means."
—Carleton College

It is the kind of information that tends to generate more heat than light. Suffice it to say, we ran across schools in which academics were rigorous and standards were high. We also encountered colleges where there was general agreement that academics were weak and faculty and students had a tacit agreement not to burden one another.

Moreover, students told us almost universally that they worked hard, or thought they did. An overwhelming 87 percent said so, up from 81 percent in 1976 and only 49 percent in 1969. In almost equal proportion, 83 percent of students told us they considered themselves to be intellectuals as well, a jump of 19 percentage points since 1976 (Undergraduate Surveys, 1969, 1976, 1993). This is remarkable, since this is a generation that overwhelmingly rejects the notion of learning for learning's sake. Their educational goals are clearly instrumental. So hard work equals an intellectual orientation. Time spent means achievement attained. There is no distinction between quantity and quality.

Nonetheless, we managed to locate a pretty good barometer for measuring intellectual orientation: the baseball cap. A woman at a selective university, struggling with the workload in its pre-med program, rolled her eyes and explained its significance this way: "The number of baseball caps in a given class is in inverse proportion to the academic rigor of the course." A dean of students at a smaller school summarized the scene on his campus in a similar manner: "C students wear baseball caps forward; D students wear them backwards."

Baseball caps or not, the hard work in which students are engaged is paying off in the currency of choice: grades. Only 7 percent of undergraduates say they don't care what grades they receive. Although they express a good deal of ambivalence about how accurately grades reflect their achievements (saying it is possible to get good grades without understanding the material), only a small number (21 percent) agree with their counterparts of the 1960s, when well over half (57 percent) thought undergraduate education in America would be improved if grades were abolished (Undergraduate Surveys, 1969, 1976, 1993). Undergraduates told us they wanted high grades and felt great pressure to get them. The irony is that doing so has never been easier, thanks to grade inflation. Table 6.4 illustrates the contemporary attitude about grades.

In the last thirty years, the gentleman's C has become the gentleman's A as the percentage of C's and A's given to students in college has reversed itself. In 1969, 7 percent of all students received grades of A– or higher; by 1976, this rose to 19 percent. In 1993, the proportion increased to 26 percent. In contrast, grades of C or lower decreased over the same period from 25 percent to 13 to 9 percent (Table 6.5).

Table 6.4. Student attitudes about grades: 1969, 1976, 1993.

	Percentage agreeing		
Student attitudes	1969	1976	1993
I'm not doing as well academically as I'd like.	71	58	60
My grades understate the true quality of my work.	54	59	60
It's possible to get good grades without really understanding the material.	44	61	59
Undergraduate education in America would be improved if grades were abolished.	57	32	21
I really don't care what grades I get.	12	11	7

Source: Undergraduate Surveys (1969, 1976, 1993).

Table 6.5. Cumulative grade point average reported
by undergraduates: 1969, 1976, 1993.

	Percentage reporting		
Cumulative GPA	1969	1976	1993
Disaggregated			
A+ or A	2	8	13
A–	5	11	13
B+	11	18	18
B	17	22	21
B–	19	15	13
C+	23	15	12
C	18	10	7
C– or below	7	3	2
Aggregated			
A– or higher	7	19	26
C or below	25	13	9

Source: Undergraduate Surveys (1969, 1976, 1993).

Grade inflation is not a new phenomenon, nor is it confined to postsecondary education. Its roots appeared with the progressive rhetoric of the 1960s. In the latter part of that decade, the effects of the war in Vietnam (especially fear of the draft) were also influential factors. Today there are many reasons for grade inflation. The increasing proportion of students of nontraditional age—usually serious minded and often very focused—plays a part. Collegiate fears of student attrition are another factor. So too is the rise of merit scholarships in higher education that require students to maintain high grade-point averages to keep their scholarships. Worries about litigation by students is yet another element. Finally, the definition of success in graduate schools, where A's and B's are the only satisfactory grades, is trickling down to the undergraduate level, encouraging faculty to use the same standards for both.

Despite grade inflation, or maybe because of it, academic dishonesty is an issue on campus, though not so large a one as media coverage would have us believe. Widespread collegiate cheating as reported periodically by the press was not found in this study. Students don't need to cheat to pass their courses. However, approximately one-fifth (21 percent) of all student affairs officers told us of increases over the last decade in reported incidents of cheating or plagiarism, more at four-year schools (30 percent) than two-year colleges (12 percent) (Student Affairs Survey, 1997), and 8 percent of students asserted that some forms of cheating are necessary to get the grades they want. There is variation, but not a great deal, among different campus constituencies, as Table 6.6 illustrates.

The percentage of students who say they cheat has been almost constant since 1969; in fact, it dipped by a little less than 1 percentage point between 1976 and 1993 (Undergraduate Surveys, 1969, 1976, 1993). What is shocking, however, is that more than three out of four deans of students say students are less likely to view plagiarism as wrong (Student Affairs Survey, 1997). As one dean put it, "Twenty years ago honesty was not such a big problem. . . . Now, what is right changes with the situation." This is likely a

Table 6.6. Students reporting that "some forms of cheating are necessary to get the grades I want," by institutional type, attendance, gender, resident status, and age: 1993.

Student characteristics	Percentage reporting
All students	8
Type of institution	
Two-year colleges	5
Four-year institutions	9
Universities	11
Attendance	
Full-time	9
Part-time	3
Gender	
Men	10
Women	5
Resident status	
Residence hall or fraternity	11
Commuter	6
Age	
25 or younger	10
Over 25	3

Source: Undergraduate Survey (1993).

reflection of the enormous pressure to succeed and the terrible fear of failure students feel. Absolutes with regard to honesty and integrity are becoming much more relative. The expression "Whatever," which has become almost a mantra for college students, captures this reality. There isn't much they can count on.

Obstacles

Despite the ease with which students seem to attain good grades, many face high academic hurdles, which makes the good grades even more perplexing. Students are coming to college less well prepared than in the past. As a result, there is a growing need for remediation. Nearly three-fourths (73 percent) of student affairs officers reported an increase within the last decade in the proportion of students requiring remedial or developmental education at two-year (81 percent) and four-year (64 percent) colleges (Student Affairs Survey, 1997). Today, nearly one-third (32 percent) of all undergraduates reported having taken a basic skills or remedial course in reading, writing, or math, up from 29 percent in 1976 (Undergraduate Surveys, 1976, 1993). Despite high aspirations, a rising percentage of students are simply not prepared for the rigors of academe. "People who told me college is easy should be shot," wailed a student at the Illinois Institute of Technology. In 1995, more than three-fourths of all colleges and universities offered remedial reading, writing, or math courses. Between 1990 and 1995, 39 percent of institutions reported that enrollments in these areas had increased, versus 14 percent citing declining enrollments (U.S. Department of Education, 1996d).

"Faculty are astounded at the students' lack of knowledge," admitted a student at Tunxis Community College. According to the Higher Education Research Institute, less than one-quarter (24 percent) of college and university faculty would characterize students as "well prepared academically," while less than half (48 percent) gave their students even a "satisfactory" or "very satisfactory" rating in terms of their quality (Sax, Astin, Arredondo, and Korn, 1996). Our own surveys showed that 45 percent of faculty feel less comfortable with students today than in the past. This feeling is more pronounced at four-year schools (53 percent) than at two-year colleges (37 percent) (Student Affairs Survey, 1997).

There is another hurdle even more daunting than remediation: the widening gap between the ways in which students learn best and the ways in which faculty teach. According to research by Charles Schroeder of the University of Missouri-Columbia, more than half of today's students perform best in a learning situation characterized by "direct, concrete experience, moderate-to-high degrees of structure, and a linear approach to learning. They value the practical and the immediate, and the focus of their perception is primarily on the physical world." Three-quarters of faculty, on the other hand, "prefer the global to the particular, are stimulated by the realm of concepts, ideas, and abstractions, and assume that students, like themselves, need a high degree of autonomy in their work." In short, students are more likely to prefer concrete subjects and active methods of learning. By contrast, faculty are predisposed to abstract subjects and passive learning. The result, says Schroeder, is frustration on both sides and a tendency for faculty to interpret as deficiencies what may simply be "natural" differences in learning patterns of students (Schroeder, 1993, p. 25).

This mismatch may cause faculty to think that every year students are less well prepared, and students to think their classes are incomprehensible. On the faculty side, this is certainly the case. The 1997 Student Affairs Survey revealed that at 74 percent of colleges and universities, faculty complaints about students were on the rise. There is little difference at two-year (72 percent) and four-year (77 percent) colleges.

This, in part, explains why students are taking longer to complete college. Less than two out of five are able to graduate in four years (Astin, Tsui, and Avalos, 1996). Twenty-eight percent now require a fifth year to earn a baccalaureate (U.S. Department of Education, 1996a). The fact of the matter is that obtaining the baccalaureate degree in four years is an anomaly today, particularly at public and less selective institutions. Indeed, 46 percent of colleges and universities report a lengthening of the time to earn a degree during the 1990s, with the rise higher at two-year (48 percent) than at four-year schools (43 percent) (Student Affairs Survey, 1997).

Among the reasons for this trend toward more-than-four-year degrees are the increasing numbers of students attending school part-time and the rising proportion of students who work long hours. Other possible reasons may include the increasing time required for remediation; the quickly rising cost of college tuition; and the fact that colleges and universities, particularly large public universities, are increasingly making students stay on longer by offering required courses in inadequate numbers, at inconvenient times, and out of sequence.

Student Satisfaction

With such a mismatch between students and their teachers, one might expect students to think of college as a fairly awful interlude in their lives. This is not the case. The vast majority attest to being satisfied with their college overall and would rather be going to college now than doing anything else (Undergraduate Survey, 1993). These figures show a steady rise, even from the high levels of satisfaction in 1976, as Table 6.7 shows.

As for the quality of teaching at their institutions, students are even more pleased. Despite a sea of complaints in the press about the quality of college teaching, students interviewed on our site visits singled out faculty over and over again as being caring and anxious to help. "It's difficult to fail courses here," said one young woman at Catholic University. "If teachers see you are having problems, they will help you."

Her comments are borne out by national statistics. The student survey shows that nearly two-thirds of undergraduates (65 percent) think there are faculty who take a special personal interest in their students' academic progress. More than one-half report having

Table 6.7. College student satisfaction: 1969, 1976, 1993.

Student attitude	Percentage agreeing		
	1969	1976	1993
Satisfied with your college overall	62	71	79
Would rather be going to college now than doing anything else	69	69	75
Satisfied with the teaching at your college	67	72	81

Source: Undergraduate Surveys (1969, 1976, 1993).

studied with professors who greatly influenced their academic careers or to whom they have felt free to turn for advice on personal matters (Undergraduate Survey, 1993). Over and over again, students mentioned ways in which faculty had reached out to them personally. A senior raved about a favorite chemistry prof who attends her diving meets as well as acting as teacher, graduate school adviser, mentor, and personal role model—all in addition to pursuing research involving Fourier transform microwave spectroscopy. Another student, at Morris Brown College, was humbled and grateful as he told the story of a faculty member who had helped him with his tuition payment until a grant arrived. "Many faculty and staff are viewed as mothers, fathers, sisters, and brothers," he added.

For students, there is an objective as well as emotional payoff to faculty-student interaction. Research has shown, not surprisingly, a positive association between academic achievement and hours per week spent talking with faculty outside of class (among other variables), and between retention (ultimately, degree completion) and a student-oriented faculty (Astin, 1993). Despite the wide variation in the cultures of our nation's academic institutions, the value of human connection remains important.

Students are also satisfied with the curriculum at their colleges, as shown in Table 6.8. On matters of curricular structure, course content, and educational relevance, there is fairly general agreement that colleges and universities are right on target. In comparison with their predecessors of the 1960s, fewer students are interested in seeing things change.

This is not to say they see no room for improvement. Desire for courses examining other cultures and for a period of community service as a requirement for graduation receives significant support. The belief that teaching effectiveness, not publications, should be the primary criterion for the promotion of faculty remains almost universal (Undergraduate Survey, 1993).

Student satisfaction with undergraduate education is amazingly high. Most individuals would not change it very much or at all and

Table 6.8. Student opinions on various educational practices: 1969, 1976, 1993.

	Percentage agreeing		
Individual practice	1969	1976	1993
Teaching effectiveness, not publications, should be the primary criterion for promotion of faculty.	96	94	91
Undergraduate education would be improved if all students were required to take courses examining other cultures.	—	—	59
Undergraduate education would be improved if students were required to spend a year in community service in the United States.	—	—	41
Undergraduate education would be improved if there were less emphasis on specialized training and more on broad liberal education.	40	31	31
Much of what is taught at my college is irrelevant to what is going on in the outside world.	42	29	28
Undergraduate education would be improved if all courses were elective.	53	35	22

Source: Undergraduate Surveys (1969, 1976, 1993).

are glad to be going to college rather than doing anything else. Although they don't believe a college degree guarantees a good job, neither do they believe you can get one without college. Nowhere are graduates saying they have regretted searching for "insurance" and taking out a policy that provides protection for the future. So even if colleges are not meeting the social expectations of students, they are doing an excellent job of satisfying their academic wishes.

In sum, their academic wishes are aimed at preparation for a career. This vocational orientation is reflected in their choice of college, their majors, and their long-term educational aspirations. More are striving for entrance to graduate or professional school, with financial success the hoped-for payoff. Most students work hard, or think they do, but tend to confuse hard work with intellectualism. High grades are the reward universally sought and fairly easily obtained, thanks in large part to grade inflation, a trend that has continued unabated since the 1960s.

But high academic achievement comes at a time when, for many, there are serious obstacles as well. More students are in need of remedial education and often do not learn best in the ways faculty prefer to teach. Frustrations run high. Nevertheless, student satisfaction with the academic experience, and with faculty in particular, has never been stronger. Most feel they have taken the first steps to ensuring future success. They plan to follow the advice of the Texas and Oregon students who said "Stay focused" and "Chase your dream."

7

The Future

Doing Well or Doing Good

> . . . And they wonder why those of us in our twenties
> refuse to work an eighty-hour week just so we can
> afford to buy their BMWs, and why we aren't inter-
> ested in the counterculture that they invented, as if
> we did not see them disavow their revolution for a
> pair of running shoes. But the question remains:
> What are we going to do now? How can we repair
> all the damage we inherited? Fellow graduates, the
> answer is simple. The answer is . . . the answer is
> . . . I don't know.
>
> Commencement address by Lelaina Pierce,
> lead character in Reality Bites (1984)

No generation has wanted to believe in the American dream more than current undergraduates.

They want good jobs. As shown in Table 7.1, 58 percent are aiming for careers in the platinum professions of business, law, medicine, and technology, an 8-percentage-point increase since the 1970s (Undergraduate Survey, 1993).

They want successful relationships; 92 percent say it is important for them to have a good relationship or marriage (Undergraduate Survey, 1993).

Table 7.1. Student career plans in selected fields: 1976, 1993.

Professional fields	Percentage choosing	
	1976	1993
Business, public relations, management	22	23
Medicine and health	16	17
Engineering, computers, other technical	10	13
Elementary or secondary teaching	12	11
Law	4	7
Human or social services	8	7
College teaching, research	5	6
Arts (visual and performing)	3	5
Writing, journalism, broadcast media	2	5
Agriculture, conservation, ecology	2	4
Homemaker (full-time)	1	2

Source: Undergraduate Surveys (1976, 1993).

They want children; 78 percent want to have a family, which is a 4-percentage-point increase since 1976 (Undergraduate Survey, 1993).

They want money and material goods; 75 percent of undergraduates say it is essential or very important for them to be very well off financially, a gain of more than 12 percentage points since 1979 (Astin, Parrott, Korn, and Sax, 1997; Undergraduate Survey, 1993).

They expect to be at least as well off as their parents. So say 72 percent of undergraduates; in focus group interviews, an even higher proportion said they expect to be happier than their parents (Undergraduate Survey, 1993; Campus Site Visits, 1993).

When asked to explain why they anticipated doing as well as or better than their parents, they listed several advantages their youth afforded them in comparison with what their parents had known as young people. "My father sent all his kids to college. I got a good start my father never had," asserted a student at Manhattan College. Another, at the University of Colorado, remarked: "I've already done better [than my parents]. I've already surpassed or equaled them educationally. I've done as much professionally." A third, at the University of Northern Iowa, speculated on personal as well as professional advantages: "I have higher career goals and aspirations. I will be more mobile. I want a better relationship with a spouse."

Despite these high expectations, this generation of students is deeply ambivalent. Their hopes of achieving their dreams are limitless, but their fears of the impossibility are omnipresent. They are at once energized and enervated.

Hopes

Students were asked whether they were optimistic or pessimistic about the future. Almost nine out of ten (88 percent) said they were optimistic about their personal futures. This represents a 3-percentage-point decline over the previous study but is still an astoundingly high percentage (Undergraduate Surveys, 1976, 1993). Again and again, students professed unlimited possibilities:

"I'll go places."

"Nothing is stopping me."

"My parents raised me to know I can do anything."

"God has a plan for me and it will be fulfilled, and that means it has to be the best plan for my life."

"I can do anything."

"I know I will be happy. A year ago I was shot in the chest and thought I would die. Now I know how precious life is, and I will be happy."

"I'm very optimistic."

"I have a strong sense of self. I'm blessed with abilities in different areas but still do a lot and have faith that I'm making it."

"My life is mine and I can do with it what I want. My life is headed into the sun."

Their optimism goes hand in hand with a fundamental belief in rock-bottom American values as old as Ben Franklin and the Puritan colonists. Nearly four out of five undergraduates (79 percent) believe that hard work always pays off (Undergraduate Survey, 1993). They put it this way:

"I can do anything I work hard for."

"I have always been able to do what I want to do if I work hard."

"If you work hard, the only limits are lack of imagination and desire."

"In America, hard work is what counts."

It would be inaccurate to say all undergraduates felt this way. In almost every focus group, there were undergraduates who rejected the notion entirely, saying "It's who you know," "The playing field isn't level," "The deck is stacked," and "It's a myth that hard work pays off." Often they named their own group as being particularly disadvantaged: whites don't have a chance anymore, blacks are discriminated against, women are excluded, people from the Middle East are treated worse than others. But overwhelmingly, students thought they could succeed as individuals if they worked hard enough. This was particularly true of foreign students. What they said amounted to almost a shared mantra: "America is a land of unlimited opportunity. Americans don't know how good they have it compared to other countries; I am not from this country and I know it is the best place in the world to live."

The only real subject of debate for undergraduates was what personal success meant. They were torn between doing well and doing good, that is, between having material resources and helping others. As noted, students overwhelmingly wanted to be very well off financially, but simultaneously a whopping 95 percent of undergraduates also said it was important to them to do good and help others. Five out of eight students wanted a career that would make a meaningful social contribution (Undergraduate Survey, 1993). One student explained: "For my generation, teaching is the equivalent of the Peace Corps," meaning a low-paying job that promised to make an important social contribution. Students viewed doing well and doing good as opposing goals. They generally believed that socially meaningful careers paid low salaries. High-paying jobs were viewed as antithetical to doing good, though an occasional student would cite an exception. One said that opening a productive manufacturing plant in the rust belt was the most altruistic job he could imagine. He may be right.

Students regularly offered advice on how to do well and do good simultaneously, or at least serially:

"Doing good is rewarded by doing well."

"My father is a role model. He has been successful in business but doesn't shut himself off. He brings home homeless people. He does good stuff. You can do both."

"You have to reach a certain level of economic well-being before doing good. You don't see hungry people able to make these changes."

"No, you can't do a lot without money."

"I can give time, someday money. You give financially and then, eventually, spiritually."

"I look in the mirror each morning and think how much my parents have sacrificed so that I can get an education. I see that there is no room for the weak. You cannot be effective unless you're a world shaker. Everything I do has to have an impact."

The problem was that in practice students generally could not figure out how to do both at the same time.

A particularly poignant conversation on this subject occurred in a focus group at the University of the District of Columbia. There was general agreement among the fourteen participants that they wanted to be materially successful and give something back to the generally poor black communities from which they came. The majority of the group, like their peers at colleges across the country, were currently involved in community service projects.

The interviewer asked the group how they were going to accomplish both of their goals. One student said she was going to become a lawyer and work in a major law firm. Then she was going to help the community. She spoke of giving legal help, money, and time. The rest of the group jumped on her immediately, saying, "What are you going to do, drive up in your Beemer and say I'm here to help?" They went on to say that law firms would not like to have her spending so much time away from the office with poor people who could not pay their fees. They said she would be too busy at her job to find time for the community; they claimed she could no longer be part of it. She would change personally and lose touch with the community; she would live elsewhere and would need all of her money to support "a rich suburban apartment, her wardrobe, Beemer, and family."

The would-be lawyer began by rebutting each charge. First, she laughed at them. Then she yelled at them. Finally, looking beaten, she threw up her hands and agreed with the group. She said she didn't know what to do. But no one else did either. The idea of returning to the community after college and then attending professional school was dismissed as unlikely, as was the possibility of staying in the community and taking a professional job. Making room in a professional career for a few hours each week of community service—tutoring, working in a clinic, helping out at a shelter—seemed trivial to the group.

Ultimately, the group could figure out no way to do both meaningfully. They did not want to give up on material success, nor did they want to surrender their social responsibilities. They rejected both extremes. They did not need to be one of the Fortune 500, and they did not want to become Mother Teresa. They wanted balance but had no idea how to achieve it. They did not want to choose one over the other—doing well or doing good—but ultimately they saw no other possibility, particularly since the more appealing choice was to do well. Above all, they feared they might get neither. The conversation was by turns intense, loud, angry with outbursts, and then quiet. The tension between doing well and doing good was mirrored in most of our focus group discussions.

Fears

In challenge to this generation's hope and their almost desperate desire to embrace the American dream is a tide of fear, flowing from seemingly every aspect of their lives. There is nothing tangible for them to hold onto. Elements of this fear have been described in each previous chapter.

Yes, current undergraduates are more optimistic about the future of the nation than their predecessors. They did say things like, "I guess I am an optimist. The government stinks, but I believe in the people and think we will be OK." They tell of the country's historic ability "to dig its way out of holes." They share the public's belief that America is exceptional. A recent Times Mirror survey reported that 68 percent of Americans believe "we can find a way to solve our problems and get what we want," and 62 percent "don't believe there are limits to growth in this country today" (Times Mirror Center for the People and the Press, 1994, p. 27).

Yet they temper these beliefs with worries about government: Congressional gridlock, the political systems at the national and local level, the motives and abilities of politicians, and the lack of real leaders in the country. They see almost insurmountable economic problems: the enormous national debt, the state of the economy, the scarcity of good jobs, rising poverty rates, unemployment, and the burden of entitlement programs. They speak of an endless array of social problems: homelessness, drugs, broken families, hunger, health care, violence, poor schools, and AIDS. They talk of deep and intractable divisions in the country, based on race, religion, gender, sexual orientation, and political persuasion. They have cataclysmic visions of the future of the environment. Their fears go beyond the borders of the country to include tribalism, war, terrorism, nuclear proliferation, economic competition, and genocide. Despite this generation's professed optimism, our conversations with students focused much more on their worries than on their hopes about society:

> "The great debt of the U.S. is worrisome. It has damaged the U.S. economically and politically."

> "I am patriotic, and it bothers me that we are second fiddle to Japan and Germany."

> "I'm really nervous about the international situation; it's really chaotic. There are a lot of people who hate America."

> "There are sacrifices that have to be made to make society right, and I'm afraid the people will not make them. This is especially true of the environment."

> "Things are falling apart. Schools are falling apart. I see more and more problems."

> "I'm pessimistic when I'm looking outside at the educational problems."

> "I'm worried that by the year 2000, 60 percent of the population may have AIDS."

> "I was very promiscuous as a teenager and AIDS lives like a dark shadow over me. I keep having myself tested and I'm negative, but I'm afraid."

> "Society is against me. Racism will hurt my future."

"We blacks don't know how to channel our anger."

"All good things are becoming politically correct."

"The values of society are not very strong."

"I think we're falling, falling, falling. There's not much to catch us."

"We live in a post-Christian society, and we no longer have the glue to hold society together. We will disintegrate."

"The religious right scares the living hell out of me."

"I'm very scared about the future. I'm afraid to have children."

The same is true of their private lives. Yes, the overwhelming majority of college students believe they will be successful. But their fears about relationships and romance, and whether they will be happy, were continuing themes in every focus group. Their concerns about finances were overwhelming. There was not one focus group in which students did not ask whether they would be able to repay their student loans, afford to complete college, or get a good job. The college graduate driving a cab or working at the Gap were universal anecdotes. There was more mythology here than there were concrete examples, however. College graduates being forced to drive taxis is one of the great American legends, rivaled only by the tale of George Washington and the cherry tree. It comes down to this: as a student at Portland Community College explained, "I have a dream, and if it comes true, that would be great, but I'm worried about finding the money."

Yes, they are very satisfied with college, but they are deeply concerned about its cost. Tuition prices are rising faster than inflation. More students are working, and working longer hours, to pay for higher education. Federal support for student aid has dropped sharply, and undergraduates are borrowing much more to attend college. Between 1980 and 1995, the proportion of federal financial aid given for loans versus grants nearly doubled. The number of dollars students borrowed also doubled between 1990 and 1995 (Hartle, 1994). Finally, as noted earlier, students are taking longer to graduate, on average at least a year more. Terry Hartle, vice president for governmental relations at the American Council on Education, summarized the situation this way: "The social compact that assumed that the adult generation would pay for the college education of the next generation has been shattered" (1994, p. A52).

Students raised each of these issues in our conversations. They told us of the need to drop out, stop out, and attend college part-time owing to tuition costs. They told us of the lengths they had to go to pay tuition—even giving blood. One student worked as a stripper (Gose, 1995). Another became a long-haul trucker and scheduled her classes around road trips.

At bottom, undergraduates are worried about whether we can make it as a society, and whether they can actually make it personally. In our surveys of students, the majority did say they expected to do better than their parents; but in focus groups, students regularly told us, "We're going to be the first generation who doesn't surpass our parents in making more money." "How will I buy a house?" "How will I send my kids to college?" "My dad did well and then he lost his business. I know how fast things can change."

This is a generation that is desperately clinging to its dreams, but their hope, though broadly professed, is fragile and gossamer-like. Their lives are being challenged at every turn: in their families, their communities, their nation, and their world. What is remarkable is that their hopes have not been engulfed by their fears.

8

• •

Conclusion

A Transitional Generation

The concluding chapter of *When Dreams and Heroes Died*, Levine's 1980 book based on the earlier college student studies, discussed three features of undergraduate life. It examined student characteristics that were unique to then-current undergraduates, characteristics that have been constant across generations of undergraduates, and characteristics that occurred cyclically among undergraduates, predictably following changes in the nation. Much of the character of the undergraduates of the late 1970s was explained in terms of historical cycles. Our final chapter begins where the previous volume ended. It starts with the historical cycles.

Historical Cycles Revisited

In this century, the most profound change in the character of the nation's undergraduates has been their multiplying numbers. Between 1900, when 4 percent of all eighteen-year-olds attended college, and 1997, when 65 percent of all high school graduates went on to some form of postsecondary education, the nation moved from what has been characterized as elite to mass to universal higher education. As a result, college students have come to look more and more like the rest of the country. As the nation changes in character, college students change in character.

The changes in both occur cyclically. Societies are a lot like people. They go through periods of wakeful, strenuous, and even frenetic activity, and then they must rest. A period of waking, a period of rest, a period of waking, a period of rest . . . the cycle goes on and on. In this century, war has been the dividing line, marking the end of wakefulness—a final outpouring of frenzied activity— and the beginning of rest—the onset of exhausted slumber.

Periods of waking are change oriented and reform minded. They are times when the dominant focus of the country is on community. Indeed, they could be called *periods of community ascendancy*. These periods emphasize duty to others, responsibility, the need to give, and the commonalities all Americans share. They are at once future oriented and ascetic. In this century, there have been three periods of community ascendancy: the Progressive Era, from the turn of the century through World War I; the Roosevelt to Great Depression era, from 1932 through World War II; and the 1960s, actually from the late 1950s through the Vietnam War. These periods have seen the election of progressive presidents: Theodore Roosevelt, William Howard Taft, Woodrow Wilson, Franklin Roosevelt, Harry Truman, John Kennedy, and Lyndon Johnson. Their administrations were activist socially, called for national improvement, and demanded cit- izen involvement. Capturing the spirit of such eras is John Kennedy's famed inaugural injunction, "Ask not what your country can do for you—ask what you can do for your country."

In contrast, periods of rest occurred after World War I, World War II, and Vietnam. These are times in which people are tired, having been asked in previous years to give and give more, and, finally, if necessary, to give lives—their own, those of family mem- bers, or their friends'—to fight a war. People are weary and want a break. Thoughts and actions that were directed outward turn inward to concerns that have been neglected: to getting one's life and the lives of one's family in order. The focus shifts from the community to the individual. These times can be called *periods of individual ascendancy*. They tend to be present oriented rather than future ori- ented. They are more hedonistic than ascetic, more concerned with individual rights than community responsibility, more rooted in getting than in giving, and more focused on self than on others. In such times, the nation has elected presidents (such as Warren Harding, Calvin Coolidge, Herbert Hoover, Dwight Eisenhower, Richard Nixon, Ronald Reagan, and George Bush) who champion the individual and oppose big government that places large burdens on its citizens. President Reagan caught the mood of those times when he said, "We are going to put an end to the notion that the American taxpayer exists to fund the American government. The federal government exists to serve the American people. . . . Work and family are at the center of our lives" (Reagan, 1985a, p. 268). Reagan called for an end of government that "sees people only as members of groups" in favor of government that "sees all the people of America as individuals" (Reagan, 1985b, p. 310). With the exception of the Harding administration, which promised "a return to normalcy," periods of individual ascendancy have been associated with a president's name, not a motto or a call to action, suggesting a social crusade. Their theme has been less government, less social control, and more individual freedom (Figure 8.1).

As Ernest Boyer and Arthur Levine have written, this movement back and forth between periods of individual and community ascendancy is a reflection of what John Locke called the social contract. All the members of a society are bound together by a tacit agreement, a compact among the individuals, in which they cede a portion of their autonomy for what is defined as the greater good. In exchange, they receive common services, protections, and agreed-upon freedoms.

The history of all societies is a continuing effort to find the perfect balance between the community and the individual. Societies move first in one direction, then the other, in the search for that balance. They overcompensate in both directions, and correct the balance by moving in the opposite direction. When too great an emphasis is placed on the community, individuals feel herded, smothered, and restrained. They lament the lack of privacy and the intrusion of social obligations. They then demand the opportunity to express their

Figure 8.1. Changes in the national mood: 1900–1998.

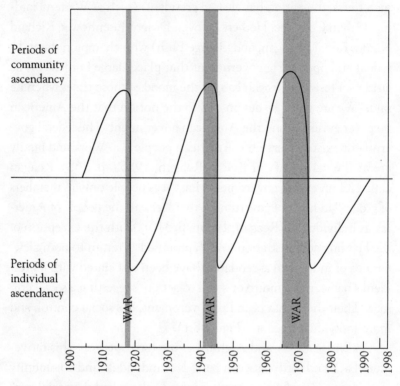

Source: Adapted from Levine (1980, p. 120).

individuality and uniqueness. In contrast, when the pendulum swings too far toward individualism and independence, people are apt to feel alone and isolated in an apathetic and uncaring world. In response, they move in the opposite direction, seeking to renew ties with their fellow human beings (Boyer and Levine, 1981).

This perennial tension between the individual and the community is mirrored in changes in the character of college students. Indeed, colleges, like all other social institutions, and undergraduates, like the rest of the population, follow the cycles of community and individual ascendancy.

During periods of individual ascendancy, students are less activist than in periods of community ascendancy. Figure 8.2 plots the

Figure 8.2. Student activism and changing national moods: 1900–1998.

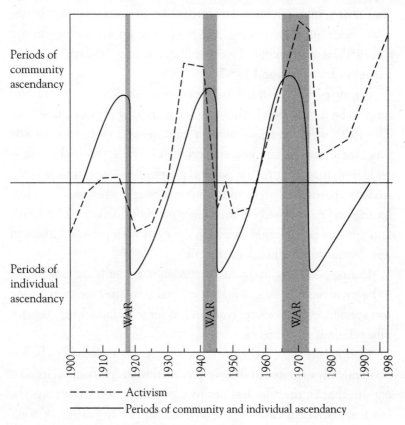

Periods of
community
ascendancy

Periods of
individual
ascendancy

WAR   WAR   WAR

1900 1910 1920 1930 1940 1950 1960 1970 1980 1990 1998

– – – – – Activism
————— Periods of community and individual ascendancy

Source: Adapted from Altbach (1974, p. 8).

extent of student activism from 1900 to 1998, based on a number of studies of student activism, particularly those of Philip Altbach.

During periods of individual ascendancy, student politics is more centrist and conservative. Ideological and political interest is relatively low. The proportion of undergraduates who are politically far right, far left, or adherents of ideologies of any type decreases. Isolationism grows and international concern declines during such times.

During periods of individual ascendancy, students are more socially rather than intellectually active. Membership in fraternities and sororities rises. Sports and intercollegiate athletics grow in popularity. Drinking increases. Fads are more likely to occur: flag-pole sitting, mah-jongg, and marathon dance contests in the 1920s; panty raids, piano wrecking, and telephone booth stuffing during the 1950s; and streaking, skateboarding, hacking, "Dallas," and toga parties in the 1970s and 1980s.

During periods of individual ascendancy, student social attitudes tend to be more liberal, allowing for increased personal freedom. The 1920s were the age of women smoking and voting for the first time, increased sexual freedom, and Freud. The 1940s and 1950s—aside from inaugurating the pill and panty raids—were a time when students, particularly returning veterans, fought strenuously against hazing and rules based on the *in loco parentis* doctrine. The 1970s and 1980s were a period in which concern with personal freedom was perhaps the hallmark of the era.

During periods of individual ascendancy, students are more likely to be involved in religious activities, and campuses are more prone to experience religious revivals and to serve as launching pads for new religious movements.

During periods of individual ascendancy, students tend to be less academically oriented and less concerned with "relevance" in education; that is, they are less desirous of instruction that treats the burning social concerns of the day, in contrast to periods of community ascendancy.

During periods of individual ascendancy, students are more committed to the material aspects of the American dream and believe more strongly in their likelihood of attaining them.

During periods of community ascendancy, trends move in exactly the opposite directions. In this context, current undergraduates do not fit into traditional cycles as well as their predecessors did. Indeed, the students of the Progressive Era, the 1930s, and the 1960s exhibited in general the characteristics of periods of community ascendancy. The undergraduates of the 1920s, 1940s, 1950s, and the seventies and eighties showed the characteristics associated with periods of individual ascendancy.

A Time of Discontinuity

The 1992 presidential election should have marked a transition from a period of individual to community ascendancy. The Reagan and Bush years drew to a close and a progressive Democrat entered the White House. But this is not what happened.

The reason is that, in the words of Rip Van Winkle, "everything's changed." The periodic oscillations from individualism to community are a phenomenon only of mature or very stable societies. They are a mechanism for maintaining the health of society by continually finding the appropriate balance between common goals and personal needs. In this manner, the competing demands of the individual and the community can both be met. This juggling act is what keeps society from flying apart and allows it to carry out business as usual under ordinary circumstances.

However, there are rare times in the history of a society in which rapid and profound change occurs. The change is so broad and so deep that the routine and ordinary cycles of readjustment cease. There is a sharp break between the old and the new. It is a time of discontinuity. In the history of this country, there have been two such break points.

The first was the Industrial Revolution, which began in earnest in the first decades of the nineteenth century. It brought about a transformation in the United States from an agricultural to an industrial society. For those who lived through it, everything appeared to be in flux. The nation's economy was turbulent and uncertain, with wide swings both up and down. New technologies with the capacity to remake the nation's daily life, ranging from steamboats and canals to railroads and mechanized factories, were burgeoning. Old industries were dying, and new industries were being born. Demographics were shifting dramatically as the population moved west and south, from rural to urban areas. Large numbers of immigrants, with relatively little formal education, were coming to America. All of the country's major social institutions—church, family, government, work, and media—were being transformed. Reflecting on the vastness of the changes, Henry Adams concluded that "the old universe was thrown into the ash heap and a new one created" (Adams, [1918] 1931, p. 5).

Adams's assessment was very close to the mark. The effects of industrialization have been well documented. Among the consequences are family disorganization, attenuation of kinship ties, and a splintering of connections between generations. Mate selection and marital patterns are retarded. Gender roles change. Homogeneity gives way to heterogeneity. Apathy and alienation grow. New and higher literacy levels are required to function in society, causing sharp differentiation in the wealth and status of the populace. Mass communication expands, and isolation within society declines. Interest groups and associations multiply (Moore, 1963).

As the reader will have guessed, the second break point or time of discontinuity is occurring now. As shown in Chapter One, the United States is currently undergoing profound demographic, economic, global, and technological change. Demographically, the U.S. population is aging, changing color, coming from other countries, and redistributing itself across the country at astounding rates.

Economically, change is occurring at what appears an even quicker pace. In one generation, the United States has moved from being the largest creditor to the largest debtor nation in the world. In one generation, the country has gone from having a resource-rich government to a resource-poor one. In six generations, the nation has shifted from a rural and agrarian society to an urban and industrial nation and then to a suburban and information-based global economy. The signs of the change are all around us: the ailing farms in the heartland, a rust belt dotting the Midwest and East, roller-coastering high-technology centers, and troubled inner cities.

Globally, the United States has become a part of an interconnected world. Four of the last five presidential elections were determined by events in the Middle East. Creation of jobs in Japan and Korea exacts a price in terms of jobs in New York, Pennsylvania, and California. When countries in central Europe come apart and others in western Europe join together, the stock market plunges and surges. This interdependence is a new experience for the United States.

Technologically, our daily lives are filled with devices and realities that were the stuff of science fiction a few decades ago. The authors' grandparents were born before the airplane was invented, and our children were born after men landed on the moon. This is a dizzying rate of change.

The nature and degree of change today is very much like that of the Industrial Revolution. Henry Adams's description of his own times seems an apt characterization of ours as well. However, several important elements might be added to what Adams said. First, the razing of the old order and the building of the new may go on simultaneously, but they are not experienced that way by most people. The emerging order is unknowable and unrecognizable; it is the future. The old order appears to be falling apart; nothing works as well as it used to. The dominant emotion is necessarily one of loss. We can see that today. All of our major social institutions, which were created for an industrial society, now appear to be broken: government, education, manufacturing, health care, the family. The reaction of the nation is not one of potential and promise, but rather of loss and frustration.

Second, we name periods of profound change only in retrospect. During the antebellum period of the nineteenth century, people did not wake up in the morning and say, "No wonder the old rules seem to have been thrown out and nothing works as well as it used to; it is the Industrial Revolution!" Instead, they were confused, frustrated, angry, lost, flailing, and often failing. It was not until the 1890s that the name *Industrial Revolution* came to stick. Prior to that time, there was a plethora of possibilities to describe the massive change the nation had been through. Only when the period assumed a single agreed-upon name could the pattern of change be comprehended. This recurring process is not wholly different from our penchant for naming generations of young people.

Third, it is impossible to say with any sense of accuracy where we are or where we are going in terms of the current wave of change. To describe our society in the decades ahead is a guessing game; it is fantasy. Which of the ongoing changes is most important? Which will dominate? Will the era we are living through be called the Demographic Revolution? Perhaps the Economic Revolution? Maybe the Technological Revolution? How about the Global Revolution? No one knows, nor will anyone know for years to come. Business writer Jane Bryant Quinn put it best when she said in a 1992 conversation, "If you are not confused by what is going on today, you don't understand it."

For today's college students, this world of change dominates their lives. The cycles of community and individualism have given way to a world of unceasing, unknowable change.

This reality is compounded by the enormous size of the population attending college today. As a consequence, the benefit of a college education has diminished. When only a small proportion of an age group graduates from college, they are virtually guaranteed the best jobs a society offers. When the majority attend college, this is no longer possible. The guarantee of the best jobs expires along with the guarantee of *any* job. In short, the students who attended college at the turn of the century were shopping at the educational equivalent of Tiffany's. Today's undergraduates are at something much more akin to Kmart. The multiplication in size of the college student population means they are subject to exactly the same social forces as the rest of the nation's population. A smaller, more elite group might have been protected from the waves of change crashing upon the rest of the country. The college cohort is simply too large today to be sheltered in any fashion.

Moreover, higher education has become a mature industry. Throughout this century, higher education was a growth industry, increasing in size annually, except for wars and two years of the Depression. During that time, the sole demand of government and the public made on colleges and universities was to increase capacity—

make it possible for more and more students to enroll. Today, there are few in government who want further growth. In the state houses of America, there is no clamor to increase the proportion of college attendance to 70 or 80 percent of the age group. Even President Clinton is focusing on reducing the cost of college through tax incentives rather than increasing the pool of students attending college. As a result, government today is asking hard questions it never asked before about the appropriate size of higher education and the effectiveness and efficiency of its work.

With growth industries, the focus is on providing resources for expansion and eliminating the impediments that retard it. With mature industries, the aim is just the opposite; the goal is to control growth, reduce cost, measure achievement, and require accountability. The result is that current undergraduates are coming to college at a time in which there are fewer public financial incentives for them to attend, and there is less public support for the institutions in which they are enrolled, causing colleges to scale back their programs and staffing levels. This means that colleges are also less able to shelter or protect their students from social conditions than they were once able to.

This is a generation that is feeling the full brunt of massive social change, more so than their predecessors ever did. For instance, even at the height of the Great Depression of the 1930s, the federal government provided financial aid to colleges in order to get more students to attend. The rationale was *not* to protect students; it was to keep them out of the labor market. Nonetheless, the infusion of dollars did have a simultaneous sheltering effect on Depression-era undergraduates.

The consequence of rapid social change and shifting conditions in higher education today is a generation straddling two worlds, one dying and another being born. Each makes competing and conflicting demands on today's college generation; they are torn between both. A dying world makes them want security, and a world being born makes urgent their call for change. In the same fashion, pragmatism wrestles with idealism, doing well with doing good, and fear with hope. They are, above all else, a transitional generation, not unlike the young people of Henry Adams's day, and they are experiencing the same symptoms as did those who lived through the Industrial Revolution.

Education for a Transitional Generation

As a group, current undergraduates might be described as having the following characteristics. They are

- Frightened

- Demanding of change

- Desirous of security

- Disenchanted with politics and the nation's social institutions

- Bifurcated in political attitudes between left and right; the middle is shrinking

- Liberal in social attitudes

- Socially conscious and active

- Consumer oriented

- Locally rather than globally focused

- Sexually active, but socially isolated

- Heavy users of alcohol

- Hardworking

- Tired

- Diverse and divided

- Weak in basic skills and able to learn best in ways different from how their professors teach

- Pragmatic, career oriented, and committed to doing well

- Idealistic, altruistic, and committed to doing good

- Optimistic about their personal futures

- Optimistic about our collective future

- Desperately committed to preserving the American dream

This generation is no better and no worse than any other generation, but, like every other generation before, it is unique. As a result, this generation requires a unique brand of education that will enable it to attain its personal dreams and to serve the society it must lead. The education we offered to previous generations, whether successful or not, will not work for these students. They are different, and their times are different. Above all, current undergraduates are in need of an education that provides them with four things.

Hope

The first is hope. When we speak about hope, we do not mean the flabby or groundless, rosy-eyed, Pollyannaish brand. Rather, we mean the kind of conviction that allows a person to rise each morning and face the new day. It is the stuff Shakespeare talked of when he wrote, "True hope is swift and flies with swallow's wings; / Kings it makes gods, and meaner creatures kings" (*Richard III* 5.2.23). Current students profess to being optimistic about the future; but as discussed in Chapter Seven, that optimism is frail.

By way of example, in the course of our research we talked with a student who told us she was majoring in business. We asked how she liked it. She said she hated it. We asked what she would rather be majoring in. She said dance. We asked, Why not major in dance? She looked at us the way one would look at a dumb younger sibling and said, "Rich is nice. Poor is not nice. I want nice," and she walked off. We had no answer that day, but over time we have thought about that student a lot. She gave up all of her dreams to study a subject she hated. If she follows a career that flows from her major, she will probably dislike that too. The saddest, saddest part of the story is that she did not have to make the choice she did. This student may not have become a professional dancer, but she could manage a dance company, or be a dance teacher, or a critic, or perhaps operate a store selling dance equipment. The tragedy of the story is not that she made a bad selection. It is that the young woman gave up her hope. It was so tenuous that she dared not hold onto it. In one form or another, this was true of many of the students we interviewed.

Responsibility

The second attribute is responsibility. Despite all we said about the adversities this generation is facing, current college students are still among the most fortunate people in the world. They owe something to others. Indeed, they are more involved in service activities than their predecessors, but at the same time they are not convinced that they can both do good and do well. Many feel that when it comes to security and responsibility, a choice must be made.

At a New England liberal arts college, all first-year students were required to participate in an exercise called "Freshman Inquiry." Students were required to prepare an essay talking about what they had learned and not learned in college so far, their hopes and aspirations for the future, and how they planned to use the remainder of their college education. After the essay was written, each student met with a panel composed of a faculty member, an administrator, and a fellow student to discuss it. One student submitted an essay to a panel, saying when she grew up she wanted to be CEO of a multinational corporation, become a U.S. senator, head a foundation that provided scholarships for college students, and work for nuclear disarmament. The student was asked what she needed out of college to accomplish all this. After a little thought, she answered, "A killer instinct." Her listeners sought clarification. She said this meant the ability to step on people or walk over them when necessary to get what she wanted. She was asked about altruism. This time she asked for clarification, and the word was defined for her. She said that was not part of her game plan. The panel reminded her of her desire to work for nuclear arms control. Surely that was altruistic. She told the panel they did not get it: "If there were a nuclear war, I would not get to be CEO of a multinational corporation." Three years later, the student graduated, plans and opinions intact. Her grades were high, and several years later she was attending one of the nation's better business schools. All of her dreams may come true, but one is forced to conclude that her college experience was inadequate. It never taught her about responsibility, what she had an obligation to do for others.

Appreciation of Differences

The third attribute is understanding and appreciation of differences. Today's undergraduates are living in a world in which differences are multiplying and change is the norm, but they attend colleges that are often segregated on the basis of differences and where relationships between diverse populations are strained. They were unable to talk about those differences in our focus group interviews. When they did talk awkwardly about them, diverse students could not even face one another. These realities were discussed in Chapter Four. It is imperative that college students learn to recognize, respect, and accept their differences.

Efficacy

The final attribute is efficacy, that is, a sense that one can make a difference. Here again, current undergraduates affirmed this belief at the highest rates recorded in a quarter century, but in focus group interviews they expressed serious doubts. It brings to mind a group we met at a well-known liberal arts college. The college had created a special program for its most outstanding seniors to prepare them for the nation's most prestigious graduate fellowships. Levine was asked to talk to the students about leadership. After a few minutes of watching the students squirming in their seats, looking out the windows, and staring at their watches, he concluded the talk was not going well.

He told the group what he suspected; they agreed. They traded hypotheses back and forth about what had gone wrong. Finally, one student said, "Life is short. This leadership stuff is bullshit. We could not make a difference even if we wanted to." Levine took a quick poll of the group to see how many agreed with the student. Twenty-two out of twenty-five hands went up.

Today's students need to believe that they can make a difference. Not every one of them will become president of the United States, but each of them will touch scores of lives far more directly and tangibly—family, friends, neighbors, and coworkers. For ill or for good, in each of those lives students will make a difference. They need to be convinced that making a difference is their birthright. They should not give it away. No one can take it away.

Preparation of a Transitional Generation

These four attributes—hope, responsibility, appreciation of differences, and efficacy—are things that people learn or fail to learn growing up. They are taught by the entire community around them: a family, a neighborhood, youth groups, schools, churches, media, and government. Collectively and individually, these institutions have failed the current generation of college students. Each has declined in influence and power, decreased in trust and public confidence, diminished in its capacity or willingness to care for children, and eroded in stature as a role model and teacher for young people. They have been unable to develop the four attributes in our college students because they themselves are lacking in the very same attributes.

A Curriculum

This failure in preparing a generation of students forces colleges into the position of having to provide "remedial" education, not in the usual sense of needing to offer courses in reading, writing, and arithmetic (though they do this too). Rather, the education is remedial in the sense of having to compensate for what the other social institutions have failed to give young people over eighteen or more years.

Today's undergraduates need an education that includes five specific elements. These ideas are not new or shocking, but the content must be different from how these areas have been generically described for the past millennium. They must be fitted to today's undergraduates and their specific needs.

Communication

The first of these elements is communication and thinking skills. At the most basic level, current students need to be fluent in two languages: words and numbers. All learning is premised on mastery of these skills. For a generation that is weak in both languages, it is essential that each be included in the college curriculum.

The enormous change in the world in which current students will live their lives also necessitates that they master what might be called transition skills. These skills could be named the three C's. *Critical thinking* is imperative in an age in which information is multiplying geometrically, ideologies masquerade as facts, and hard policy choices need to be faced. *Continuous learning,* the ability to learn independently throughout one's life, is also mandatory in an era in which the half-life of knowledge is declining precipitously and new learning technologies are burgeoning. *Creativity* is essential as well for a period in which the tried and true understandings of the past are quickly becoming aged and less useful.

As a corollary to mastering these transition skills, however, students must also understand how to access knowledge and use it effectively. Modern technology has revolutionized the process of recording, storing, and retrieving information. Learning how to access a vast body of knowledge that is constantly expanding and being revised is a critical first step in its acquisition. But the process of learning does not end there. The ability to make connections between, build on, and synthesize knowledge is crucial if purposeful learning and understanding are to take place.

For this generation of students, finding context for pieces of information is more complex than it used to be. At a time when books and libraries once provided discrete context for the information they contained, the process of acquiring and using knowledge was much simpler. Today, the contexts have changed or don't exist. For students of the 1990s, the process of acquiring pieces of information is like trying to fill a teacup with a fire hose. Using that information and knowledge effectively is the true challenge. Those who learn to think critically, learn continuously, and act creatively—those who have mastered the three C's and are able to put them to good use—have acquired techniques to enable them to convert the knowledge they acquire into value.

Human Heritage

The second element is the study of human heritage. True hope demands an understanding of the past as well as of the present. Society, in the words of Edmund Burke, is a contract, "a partnership not only between those who are living, but between those who are living, those who are dead, and those who are to be born" ([1790] 1967, p. 318). The goal for this study is not for students to memorize a list of great names and key dates, but rather to understand how societies and peoples have responded to an ever-changing economic, political, social, and technological world. Only if we can teach students about the successes and failures, the evolutions and transitions, and the rises and declines of humanity and society can their hopes and fears be realistically grounded.

In the past, this was accomplished by teaching undergraduates about the United States and the Western world. This is no longer sufficient. Today they live in an interconnected global society in which the Koran has more influence on their daily lives than the Gettysburg Address does. It is a time in which our college students draw greater inspiration from Boris Yeltsin and Nelson Mandela than from their own political leaders. It is imperative that we educate current undergraduates about humankind in the fullest sense of the term.

The Environment

The third element is education regarding the environment in which students will live their lives. This is a "green" generation, one that deeply fears the desecration of the environment. They have no confidence in the groups now controlling the environment—government, business, and the press, among others. Many have turned away from the environment writ large. Their focus is chiefly local; their vision needs to be enlarged. Even if students ultimately choose to act locally, they must think globally. This means they need to understand both the natural environment and the humanmade environment in which we live, and take responsibility for caring for each.

With regard to the natural environment, students need to become literate scientifically; they need to know the basic facts and ways of thinking that constitute science. They must come to understand the inhabitants, planet, and universe in which we live. They must be educated to serve as effective citizens for the environment, that is, learn about the public policy choices they will need to make and the criteria for making those choices.

With regard to the humanmade environment, the agenda is larger and even more difficult. Ralph Waldo Emerson wrote, "We do not make a world of our own, but fall into institutions already made and have to accommodate ourselves to them. . . ." (Emerson, 1909, p. 448). Current undergraduates are more negative about those institutions and more distrusting of their leaders than any group we have surveyed. They are rejecting both. It is essential that before turning their backs, they learn about what the range of social institutions—political, cultural, aesthetic, economic, and spiritual—is intended to accomplish. Students should learn how these institutions come into being, how they change over time, how they function and malfunction, and how they impose obligations and can be held accountable.

Individual Roles

The individual but multifaceted role that each of us plays is the fourth element in the curriculum. This is essential if students are to develop a sense of efficacy. Doing so is critical for a generation that believes that an individual can make a difference, while government is failing. It is invaluable for undergraduates who want families but have never witnessed happy marriages. It is a must for students who can't figure out whether to do well or do good. Shakespeare eloquently described this facet of our being, saying "All the world is a stage / And all the men and women merely players. / They have their entrances and their exits. / And one man in his time plays many parts" (*As You Like It* 2.7.139). Students need to know about each of those parts, all of the roles they will have to play: individual, friend, lover, family member, worker, citizen, leader, and follower. They must understand the nature of relationships, the choices they can make, the expectations associated with each role, the ways in which balance can be achieved among the various roles, and the part each role plays in creating a full and complete life. The curriculum must give them the skills, knowledge, and experience to perform each role. This is the career planning and preparation that today's students so desperately need, in its broadest and most basic form.

Values

The fifth and final element in the curriculum is values. This is critically important if students are to gain an appreciation of differences, or respect one another, or understand why cheating is wrong. But it also underlies each of the other attributes. Bertrand Russell explained the need for this fifth study when he wrote, "Without civic morality, communities perish; without personal morality, their survival has no value" (Russell, 1949, p. 70). Students must learn the meaning of values, be able to distinguish between values and facts, understand the difference between relative and absolute values, and differentiate between good, better, and best values. They also need to develop mechanisms for weighing and choosing among values. Finally, they need to comprehend how values function in our society and in their lives: the changing nature of values over time, how values fit into cultures, the place of values in an individual's life, and what happens to minority values in a society.

A Curriculum for Living

These five elements spell out a formal curriculum that colleges and universities can adopt. It differs from the traditional curriculum in that it is not rooted in the familiar disciplines and subject areas that higher education usually employs. Instead, it is grounded in the life needs of students. It is a curriculum designed specifically to prepare current undergraduates for the life they will lead and the world in which they will live. It seeks to marry intellectual vitality, which is intrinsic to academe, with the practical education students so urgently require today.

At bottom, what is being proposed is a contemporary vision of liberal education. Undergraduate education has changed dramatically over its more than three-and-a-half-century history in this country, to meet the twin needs of remaining intellectually vital and providing useful or practical education. Whenever societies change quickly, there is a tendency for the curriculum to lose these anchor points. In a short period of time, a course of study becomes anachronistic. It no longer prepares students for the world in which they will live, and it imparts an intellectual tradition that has become outdated.

In the early decades of the nineteenth century, as America under-went the Industrial Revolution, the classic collegiate curriculum faced just such a challenge. The study of the trivium and quadrivium, which had been excellent preparation intellectually and practically for a theocratic, agrarian community, no longer fit an industrializing republic. The result, after decades of innovation and experiment, was creation of a new undergraduate curriculum that would prepare its students for an industrial democracy. It is the curriculum that con-tinues to the present, rooted in a structure of courses, disciplines, spe-cialization, and breadth.

Today, as our society once again is being transformed, it is nec-essary to develop a new curriculum, an educational program that will prepare our students to live simultaneously in two societies, one dying and the other being born. Our current students are a transi-tional generation, and they need a curriculum that prepares them to assume the enormous responsibilities of building a new world while living in an old and rapidly changing society. The proposed curricu-lum is offered with the hope that it might achieve this purpose.

What is being suggested is not simply a formal set of courses. Indeed, each of the five curricular elements could be translated into a set of discrete courses. However, the five elements are interdepen-dent and overlapping. For instance, the transitional skills could be translated into three different courses, one for each of the C's. That would be a mistake. It would be preferable to teach transitional skills as part of each of the other four elements. Similarly, values could be made into a freshman seminar or the senior capstone course of the nineteenth century college, but it would be more desirable to teach values across the entire curriculum. In a like manner, learning about individual roles could be an isolated set of subjects, but in reality these roles cannot be understood without the context that studying our shared environment provides.

Moreover, the proposed curriculum is not only about subject matter and content, it is also about pedagogy. As noted earlier, there is a growing gap between how professors prefer to teach and how students best learn. This curriculum benefits from joining the two approaches, that is, marrying concrete and abstract knowledge acquired both through active and passive methods of learning. The classics need to be augmented with case studies, and the classroom needs to be supplemented with field experiences for this curriculum to work. One of the most potent approaches is to combine the very popular community service activities in which students are now involved with in-class instruction; that is, make service an integral part of the formal curriculum rather than just another extracurricular opportunity.

Furthermore, the education being proposed needs to go beyond the formal curriculum. The five elements can better be attained by infusing them throughout collegiate life. They should be underlined in the awards an institution gives, in the speakers who are invited to campus, in widely attended events such as orientation and graduation, in the publications an institution distributes, in the services students are provided, and in the activities in which students are involved. The cocurriculum is as powerful a vehicle for teaching these elements as the curriculum.

Colleges and universities cannot be expected to embrace this agenda alone. Government, churches, social organizations, and business can make an important contribution. They can do this by supporting community service programs for their constituents, members, and employees. Community service is one of the most effective methods we know for teaching hope, responsibility, appreciation of differences, and efficacy. The overwhelming majority of college students are already participating in service programs; they need to find ways to sustain their involvement beyond the college years. They also need to find ways to sustain or, better yet, enhance their sense of hope, responsibility, appreciation of differences, and efficacy after college. Without nourishment, these attributes dry up and die. With continual reinforcement, they just might empower a transitional generation and be passed on from that generation to their children.

Appendix A

Studies Used in This Report

The quantitative and qualitative data used in this book, as well as its 1980 predecessor *When Dreams and Heroes Died: A Portrait of Today's College Student*, were drawn from several sources. The authors refer to their research as Undergraduate Surveys (1969, 1976, and 1993), Student Affairs Surveys (1978, 1992, and 1997), Campus Site Visits (1979 and 1993), and Student Leaders Survey (1995). Other sources of national data were consulted as well, either to supplement the information gathered throughout these studies or to provide external confirmation of observed trends.

The Undergraduate Surveys of 1969, 1976, and 1993 examined student life on our nation's campuses. The 1969 surveys (called in the previous book "Carnegie Surveys, 1969") were conducted under the auspices of the Carnegie Commission on Higher Education with the cooperation of the American Council on Education and support from the U.S. Office of Education. They probed the opinions and experiences of sixty thousand faculty, seventy thousand undergraduates, and thirty thousand graduate students. Those of 1976 were conducted by the Carnegie Council on Policy Studies in Higher Education and involved twenty-five thousand faculty members, twenty-five thousand undergraduates, and twenty-five thousand graduate students. In both 1969 and 1976, the students surveyed included those of traditional and nontraditional age.

Following up the earlier studies, the Undergraduate Survey of 1993 was undertaken by the authors at the Harvard University Graduate School of Education. It was administered by the Opinion Research Corporation of Princeton, New Jersey, and supported by a grant from the Lilly Endowment. The survey randomly sampled ninety-one hundred traditional-age and nontraditional-age undergraduate students nationwide at institutions stratified by Carnegie type in the classification system then current: Research Universities I and II, Doctorate-Granting Colleges and Universities I and II, Comprehensive Universities and Colleges I and II, Liberal Arts Colleges I and II, and Two-Year Colleges. These included both public and private institutions. Two-thirds of the students contacted responded to the questionnaire. As in 1969 and 1976, the data obtained from this survey were weighted by Carnegie category to reflect the composition of American higher education.

College administrators' perspectives on campus life were sought as well. Three principal studies, referred to in this book as the Student Affairs Surveys (1978, 1992, and 1997), composed this second body of data, which complemented the Undergraduate Surveys described above. Like the study of students and faculty in 1976, the 1978 study of key administrative personnel (Student Affairs Survey, 1978) was conducted under the auspices of the Carnegie Council, targeting a representative sample of 586 two-year and four-year colleges and universities. Three questionnaires were sent to participating institutions, one to the president, one to an institutional research officer or similar administrator, and one to a student affairs staff member. In 1992, a similar instrument was used by the authors at the Harvard Graduate School of Education to survey the chief student affairs officers at 270 colleges and universities. To update the results of the 1992 survey, the study was repeated and a survey sent at the end of 1996 to the same institutions, which responded at a rate of 58 percent. The results were reported in 1997.

Qualitative information came from daylong campus visits to diverse two-year and four-year colleges and universities across the country. The Campus Site Visits of 1979 (referred to in the previous book as "Carnegie Study, 1979") involved twenty-six institutions that had participated in the 1978 Student Affairs Survey (called previously "Carnegie Survey, 1978"). The Campus Site Visits of 1993 took place at twenty-eight of the colleges and universities that had responded to the 1992 Student Affairs Survey:

Berkshire Community College (Pittsfield, Massachusetts)

Boston University (Boston, Massachusetts)

Carleton College (Northfield, Minnesota)

Catholic University (Washington, District of Columbia)

Concordia College (Portland, Oregon)

Drake University (Des Moines, Iowa)

Emerson College (Boston, Massachusetts)

Georgia Institute of Technology (Atlanta, Georgia)

Illinois Institute of Technology (Chicago, Illinois)

Los Angeles Valley College (Van Nuys, California)

Manhattan College (Riverdale, New York)

Morris Brown College (Atlanta, Georgia)

Oglethorpe University (Atlanta, Georgia)

Polk Community College (Winter Haven, Florida)

Portland Community College (Sylvania campus, Portland, Oregon)

Rollins College (Winter Park, Florida)

Roosevelt University (Chicago, Illinois)

St. John's University (Jamaica, New York)

Southern Methodist University (Dallas, Texas)

Tunxis Community College (Farmington, Connecticut)

University of California, Santa Barbara (Santa Barbara, California)

University of Colorado at Boulder (Boulder, Colorado)

University of the District of Columbia (Washington, District of Columbia)

University of Minnesota, Twin Cities (Minneapolis, Minnesota)

University of Northern Iowa (Cedar Falls, Iowa)

University of Texas at Arlington (Arlington, Texas)

Wayne State University (Detroit, Michigan)

Wellesley College (Wellesley, Massachusetts)

These institutions and those visited in 1979 reflect the diversity of the original sample.

At each school, the chief student affairs officer who completed the questionnaire, or a designated substitute, was interviewed. In addition, the head of student government, the campus newspaper editor, and a group of between six and ten undergraduates (chosen intentionally for diversity) were queried, using a standard list of questions. A total of 182 students in 1979 and 230 in 1993 participated in the group interviews. The researchers examined bulletin boards and posters, observed student gathering places, collected student newspapers, and frequently had the opportunity to speak with other undergraduates or staff members.

To keep the 1993 research current, the same twenty-eight institutions were contacted again via the Student Leaders Survey of 1995. Telephone conversations with a student at each institution were designed to monitor the political pulse of the student body, gather information on issues currently of concern to students, and assess any significant changes in campus activity since the interviews two years earlier.

Another major source of data used in this book is the Cooperative Institutional Research Program (CIRP). Administered by the Higher Education Research Institute (HERI) of the University of California at Los Angeles, the national longitudinal CIRP study is under the continuing sponsorship of the American Council on Education. Since 1966, a representative sample of first-time full-time freshmen has been surveyed annually. The number of colleges and universities participating annually has ranged from about four hundred to more than one thousand nationwide. Reports of the results are published each year. HERI's follow-up research on these freshmen two and four years after college entry has also been valuable. These reports and information about them are available from the Higher Education Research Institute, UCLA Graduate School of Education and Information Studies, Mailbox 951521, Los Angeles, CA 90029–1521.

Appendix B

• •

Campus Contacts

The following individuals coordinated the 1993 campus site visits and/or were the liaisons for the 1995 Student Leaders Survey:

Berkshire Community College (Pittsfield, Massachusetts)
Gary Lamoureaux
J. Jeffrey Doscher

Boston University (Boston, Massachusetts)
Wendall Norman Johnson
Mark Nohoney
Drew Kline

Carleton College (Northfield, Minnesota)
Robert Bonner
Bruce Colwell

Catholic University (Washington, District of Columbia)
Kate Zanger
Margaret M. Higgins

Concordia College (Portland, Oregon)
William Balke

Drake University (Des Moines, Iowa)
Donald Adams

Emerson College (Boston, Massachusetts)
Ron Ludman

Georgia Institute of Technology (Atlanta, Georgia)
Roger Wehrle

Illinois Institute of Technology (Chicago, Illinois)
Daniel Waldstein
Bonnie Gorman

Los Angeles Valley College (Van Nuys, California)
Mary Spangler
Samuel Mayo

Manhattan College (Riverdale, New York)
E. Joseph Lee

Morris Brown College (Atlanta, Georgia)
Sharon Walker
William Settle

Oglethorpe University (Atlanta, Georgia)
Donald Moore

Polk Community College (Winter Haven, Florida)
Angelo Pimpinelli

Portland Community College (Sylvania campus, Portland, Oregon)
Craig Bell

Rollins College (Winter Park, Florida)
Steve S. Neilson
Susan Allen
Penny Schaeffer

Roosevelt University (Chicago, Illinois)
Gregory M. Hauser
Ellen Meets-Decagny

St. John's University (Jamaica, New York)
Susan L. Ebbs
Don McNally

Southern Methodist University (Dallas, Texas)
James Caswell

Tunxis Community College (Farmington, Connecticut)
Del Higham

University of California, Santa Barbara (Santa Barbara, California)
Gladys DeNecochea
Naomi Johnson
Candi Stevenson

University of Colorado at Boulder (Boulder, Colorado)
Jean Delaney

University of the District of Columbia (Washington, District of Columbia)
Alice M. Sykes
Willis Thomas

University of Minnesota, Twin Cities (Minneapolis, Minnesota)
Marvalene Hughes
Roger Harrold
June Nobbe

University of Northern Iowa (Cedar Falls, Iowa)
Sue Follon

University of Texas at Arlington (Arlington, Texas)
Wayne Duke

Wayne State University (Detroit, Michigan)
William Markus

Wellesley College (Wellesley, Massachusetts)
Molly Campbell

References

Adams, H. *The Education of Henry Adams*. (J. T. Adams, intro.). New York: Modern Library, 1931. (Originally published in 1918.)

Adler, J. "Kids Growing Up Scared." *Newsweek*, Jan. 10, 1994, pp. 43–50.

Altbach, P. G. *Student Politics in America: A Historical Analysis*. New York: McGraw-Hill, 1974.

Alter, J. "Powell's New War." *Newsweek*, Apr. 28, 1997, pp. 28–36.

Astin, A. W. *What Matters in College? Four Critical Years Revisited*. San Francisco: Jossey-Bass, 1993.

Astin, A. W., Parrott, S. A., Korn, W. S., and Sax, L. J. *The American Freshman: Thirty Year Trends*. Los Angeles: Higher Education Research Institute, UCLA, 1997.

Astin, A. W., Tsui, L., and Avalos, J. *Degree Attainment Rates at American Colleges and Universities: Effects of Race, Gender, and Institutional Type*. Los Angeles: Higher Education Research Institute, UCLA, 1996.

Benezra, K. "Don't Mislabel Gen X." *Brandweek*, May 15, 1995, p. 32, 34.

Bennet, J. "At Volunteerism Rally, Leaders Paint Walls and a Picture of Need." *New York Times*, Apr. 28, 1997, sec. 1, p. A1.

Boyer, E. L., and Levine, A. *A Quest for Common Learning: The Aims of General Education*. Washington, D.C.: Carnegie Foundation for the Advancement of Teaching, 1981.

Burke, E. "Reflections on the Revolution in France." In R.J.S. Hoffman and P. Levack (eds.), *Burke's Politics: Selected Writings and Speeches of Edmund Burke on Reform, Revolution, and War*. New York: Knopf, 1967. (Originally published in 1790.)

Campus Site Visits, 1979, 1993. See Appendix A.

Center for the Study of the College Fraternity. *Status of the College Fraternity and Sorority*. Bloomington: Indiana University, 1992.

Cohen, J., and Krugman, M. *Generation Ecch! The Backlash Starts Here.* New York: Simon & Schuster, 1994.

Commission on Substance Abuse at Colleges and Universities. *Rethinking Rites of Passage: Substance Abuse on America's Campuses.* New York: Center on Addiction and Substance Abuse, Columbia University, 1994.

Coupland, D. *Generation X.* New York: St. Martin's Press, 1991.

Coupland, D. "Generation X'd." *Details,* June 1995, p. 72.

Deutschman, A. "The Upbeat Generation." *Fortune,* July 13, 1992, p. 42.

"E-Mail Is Becoming a Conduit of Prejudice." *New York Times,* Feb. 16, 1997, sec. 1, p. 17.

Emerson, R. W. *Journals of Ralph Waldo Emerson.* (E. W. Emerson and W. E. Forbes, eds.). Vol. 2. Boston: Houghton Mifflin, 1909.

Gallup International. *Gallup Opinion Index: Report 1969.* Princeton, N.J.: Gallup International, Inc., 1969.

Giles, J. "Generalizations X." *Newsweek,* June 6, 1994, pp. 62–72.

Goldberg, C. "Survey Reports More Drug Use by Teenagers." *New York Times,* Aug. 8, 1996, sec. 1, p. 8.

Gose, B. "New Book Shines Spotlight on Odd College Job: Stripping." *Chronicle of Higher Education,* May 26, 1995, p. A32.

Gowen, A. "Motor Voter: Goin' Mobile." *Rolling Stone,* July 8–22, 1993, p. 18.

Gross, D. M., and Scott, S. "Proceeding with Caution." *Time,* July 16, 1990, pp. 56–62.

Hanson, D. J., and Engs, R. C. "College Students' Drinking Problems: A National Study, 1982–1991." *Psychological Reports,* Aug. 1992, 71, pp. 39–42.

Harris, L., and Associates. "High Confidence in Institutions." *Harris Survey,* Mar. 5, 1979. New York: Louis Harris and Associates, Inc., 1979.

Hartle, T. W. "How People Pay for College: A Dramatic Shift." *Chronicle of Higher Education,* Nov. 9, 1994, p. A52.

Higher Education Research Institute. *The American College Student, 1991: National Norms for the 1987 and 1989 Freshman Classes.* Los Angeles: Higher Education Research Institute, UCLA, 1992.

Holland, B. "Rock the Vote Assists Passage of 'Motor' Bill." *Billboard,* June 6, 1992, p. 8, 81.

Holtz, G. T. *Welcome to the Jungle: The Why Behind Generation X.* New York: St. Martin's Press, 1995.

Hornblower, M. "Great Xpectations." *Time,* June 9, 1997, pp. 58–68.

Howe, N., and Strauss, W. "The New Generation Gap." *Atlantic Monthly,* Dec. 1992, pp. 67–89.

Howe, N., and Strauss, W. *13th Gen: Abort, Retry, Ignore, Fail?* New York: Vintage Books, 1993.

Information Please Almanac: Atlas and Yearbook 1996. (49th ed.). Boston: Houghton Mifflin, 1996.

Irving, W. *The Sketch Book.* New York: NAL/Dutton, 1961. (Originally published in 1819.)

Janoff, J. "A Gen-X Rip Van Winkle." *Newsweek,* Apr. 24, 1995, p. 10.

Kennedy, P. *Preparing for the 21st Century.* New York: Random House, 1993.

Lerner, A. "My Generation." *Tikkun,* Mar.–Apr. 1994, pp. 56–58.

Levine, A. *When Dreams and Heroes Died: A Portrait of Today's College Student.* San Francisco: Jossey-Bass, 1980.

Levine, A., and Cureton, J. S. "The Quiet Revolution: Eleven Facts About Multiculturalism and the Curriculum." *Change,* Jan.–Feb. 1992, *24*(1), pp. 24–29.

Moore, W. *Social Change.* Upper Saddle River, N.J.: Prentice Hall, 1963.

Morison, S. E. *Three Centuries of Harvard: 1636–1936.* Cambridge, Mass.: Belknap Press, 1964. (Originally published in 1936.)

Nader, R. *Unsafe at Any Speed: The Designed-In Dangers of the American Automobile.* New York: Grossman, 1965.

Peterson, R., and Bilurosky, J. A. *May 1970: The Campus Aftermath of Cambodia and Kent State.* Berkeley, Calif.: Carnegie Council on Policy Studies in Higher Education, 1971.

Presley, C. A., Meilman, P. W., and Lyerla, R. *Alcohol and Drugs on American College Campuses: Use, Consequences, and Perceptions of the Campus Environment.* Vol. 2: *1990–1992.* Carbondale: Core Institute, Southern Illinois University, 1995.

Putnam, R. "Bowling Alone: America's Declining Social Capital." *Journal of Democracy,* 1995, *6*(1), pp. 65–78.

Quinn, J. B. Conversation with Arthur Levine. Middlebury, Vt.: Middlebury College, 1992.

Reagan, R. "Acceptance Speech for the Republican Nomination, July 17, 1980." In G. Bush (ed.), *Campaign Speeches of American Presidential Candidates, 1948–1984.* New York: Ungar, 1985a.

Reagan, R. "Acceptance Speech for the Second Presidential Nomination, August 23, 1984." In G. Bush (ed.), *Campaign Speeches of American Presidential Candidates, 1948–1984.* New York: Ungar, 1985b.

Reality Bites. (D. DeVito and M. Shamberg, prod.; B. Stiller, dir.; H. Childress, screenplay.). [Videocassette]. Universal City, Calif.: Universal City Studios, 1994.

Rock the Vote. "Goals for 1996." [Information flyer]. Los Angeles: Rock the Vote, 1996.

Rock the Vote. [http://www.rockthevote.org]. Mar. 1997.

Russell, B. *Authority and the Individual*. New York: Simon & Schuster, 1949.

Saltzman, A. "The Twenty-Something Rebellion: How It Will Change America." *U.S. News and World Report*, Feb. 22, 1993, pp. 50–58.

Sanger, D. E. "Happy Days Are Here Again! Right, Voters?" *New York Times*, Apr. 28, 1996, sec. 4, p. 1.

Sax, L. J., Astin, A. W., Arredondo, M., and Korn, W. S. *The American College Teacher: National Norms for the 1995–96 HERI Faculty Survey*. Los Angeles: Higher Education Research Institute, UCLA, 1996.

Sax, L. J., Astin, A. W., Korn, W. S., and Mahoney, K. M. *The American Freshman: National Norms for Fall 1996*. Los Angeles: Higher Education Research Institute, UCLA, 1996.

Schroeder, C. C. "New Students—New Learning Styles." *Change*, Sept.–Oct. 1993, *25*(4), pp. 21–26.

Serow, R. C. "Students and Volunteerism: Looking into the Motives of Community Service Participants." *American Educational Research Journal*, 1991, *28*(3), pp. 543–556.

Smith, D. E., Wesson, D. R., and Calhoun, S. R. "Rohypnol (Flunitrazepam) Fact Sheet." [http://www.lec.org/DrugSearch/Documents/Rohypnol.html]. July 1997.

Star, A. "The Twentysomething Myth." *New Republic*, Jan. 4–11, 1993, pp. 22–25.

Stewart, A. "Youthanasia." *Chicago Tribune*, May 23, 1996, sec. 5, p. 11a.

Student Affairs Surveys, 1978, 1992, 1997. See Appendix A.

Student Environmental Action Coalition. *Sourcebook*. Chapel Hill, N.C.: Student Environmental Action Coalition, 1993.

Student Leaders Survey, 1995. See Appendix A.

Times Mirror Center for the People and the Press. *The New Political Landscape*. Washington, D.C.: Times Mirror Center for the People and the Press, 1994.

Undergraduate Surveys, 1969, 1976, 1993. See Appendix A.

Universal Almanac, 1994. Kansas City, Mo.: Andrus & McMeel, 1994.

Universal Almanac, 1997. Kansas City, Mo.: Andrus & McMeel, 1997.

U.S. Department of Commerce. Bureau of the Census. *Statistical Abstract of the United States, 1996*. (116th ed.). Washington, D.C.: U.S. Government Printing Office, 1996.

U.S. Department of Education. National Center for Education Statistics. *Youth Indicators, 1993: Trends in the Well-Being of American Youth*. Washington, D.C.: U.S. Government Printing Office, 1993.

U.S. Department of Education. National Center for Education Statistics. *Condition of Education, 1996*. (NCES 96–304). Washington, D.C.: U.S. Government Printing Office, 1996a.

U.S. Department of Education. National Center for Education Statistics. *Digest of Education Statistics, 1996*. (NCES 96–133). Washington, D.C.: U.S. Government Printing Office, 1996b.

U.S. Department of Education. National Center for Education Statistics. *National Postsecondary Student Aid Study, 1995–96: Student Financial Aid Estimates for Federal Aid Recipients 1995–96*. (NCES 97–937). Washington, D.C.: U.S. Government Printing Office, 1996c.

U.S. Department of Education. National Center for Education Statistics. *Remedial Education at Higher Education Institutions in Fall 1995*. (NCES 97–584). Washington, D.C.: U.S. Government Printing Office, 1996d.

U.S. Department of Education. National Center for Education Statistics. *Youth Indicators, 1996: Trends in the Well-Being of American Youth*. Washington, D.C.: U.S. Government Printing Office, 1996e.

Voter News Service. *National Exit Polls*. New York: Voter News Service, 1996.

Wechsler, H. "Alcohol and the American College Campus: A Report from the Harvard School of Public Health." *Change*, July–Aug. 1996, 28(4), p. 20.

Wechsler, H., Isaac, N. E., Grodstein, F., and Sellers, D. E. "Continuation and Initiation of Alcohol Use from the First to the Second Year of College." *Journal of Studies on Alcohol*, Jan. 1994, 55, pp. 41–45.

World Almanac and Book of Facts, 1997. Mahwah, N.J.: Funk & Wagnalls, 1997.

Wulf, S. "Generation Excluded." *Time*, Oct. 23, 1995, p. 86.

"Youth-Vote Group Makes Registration Laid Back." *New York Times*, Apr. 21, 1996, sec. 1, p. 28.

Zinn, L. "Move Over, Boomers: The Busters Are Here—and They're Angry." *Business Week*, Dec. 14, 1992, p. 74–79, 82.

Index